# TRUTH BE TOLD

Narratives from the Souls of Black Women

## Published by

One-L Group
8120 Sawyer Brown Road Suite 107
Nashville, Tennessee 37221
United States of America

ISBN: 978-0-9898504-4-5
Copyright © 2017 Dr. Walter Milton, Jr.

## Cover Design by

Heather R. Sanders
Lisa Petros
Jewell Winn
Walter Milton, Jr.

## Photography by

Heather R. Sanders
Taryn Andre
Brian L. Sanders (cover)

## Edited by

Norma Hedgepeth
Heather R. Sanders
Daveed and Keziah

Printed in the United States of America

# Contributors

Jasmine Sanders

Norma Hedgepeth

Lola Johnson

Candace Omar

Ayeesha Syeed

LaRhonda McLemore-Cockrell

Aretha Garr

Denise Marcia

Dr. Cierrah Perrin

Brittany Shook

Dr. Cheryl Green

JustDorcas AKA Dorcas Wiley

Justice and Somone

K. Dawn Rutledge

Willette Pare

Ava Brown

Dr. Antoinette Stroter

Carolyn Ross

Shawnta' Monique

Takyra Stephens – Chambers

Benita Thomas

Heather R. Sanders

Dr. Jewell Winn

Dr. Walter Milton, Jr.

# Acknowledgments

### Dr. Walter Milton, Jr.

I am thankful to the Most High Almighty God, for giving me the vision and ability to create this important book – the work is purposeful. I appreciate all of the individuals who participated in this project as well.

I am grateful to have been blessed with a loving family, my sons Nathaniel, Omari, Ezana and my daughter, Adrianne, who continue to exemplify unyielding support and commitment as I work diligently to achieve my desired aspirations. *Dad is always wishing the best for your lives.* My wife, Lisa has been a great mother to our four children and continues to demonstrate a great deal of sacrifice. Thank you for all that you do to keep things flowing smoothly. I am always thankful to my sisters and my brother who have helped me become the man that I am today. Over the years, I've had the privilege of inspiring and being inspired by children across the country. Thank you, Ty Watson, for being a part of our village.

My parents, Walter and Louise Milton, are no longer with us, but their spirits and love shower me every moment. They taught me the essence of what it is to be a good human being and poured a spirit of excellence into my soul. My nieces and nephews continue to be a motivation to me, and I hope that I am modeling an image that is pleasing to them. I would like to give special thanks to my sister, Dr. Jewell Winn for her commitment and dedication to excellence.

As I said before, I have been very fortunate to have had (and still have) many wonderful cheerleaders and nurturers to help me navigate life's curves and, sometimes, roadblocks. There are too many to name, but they know who they are. Again, I say thank you for being able to give me exactly what I needed, when I needed it.

Like always, I am reminded of the songwriter's words, "I don't feel any ways tired, because He has brought me too far to leave me." Thank you Yahweh – Your spirit, grace and mercy carry me through. Peace and love to my ancestors who paved the way, smoothed my path and hydrated my soul. Thanks for bending and allowing your backs to serve as bridges so that I could cross over the troubled waters. Mama, *thanks*. I will always love and cherish you. Lastly, I would like to give special recognition to the entire From The Heart International Educational Services family – peace!

# Dr. Jewell Winn

I would like to thank God for blessing and sustaining me throughout my life. Through His grace and mercy, I have been given countless opportunities to use my knowledge, skills and abilities to impact the lives of others. I am thankful to each of my Queen Sisters who had the courage to share their narratives from the heart, and my soul sister, Jasmine Sanders, for believing in the project and writing the foreword.

I am so thankful to my incredible parents, John and Katherine Green, for providing me with a foundation of love, support, and encouragement. Reflecting on all of the times that I may have performed, competed, or received awards, there was never a time that you were not present and cheering me on. You are truly my biggest fans.

To my husband Timothy, I thank you for being all that I need, to be all that I can be. For every dream, every idea, and every undertaking – you were there by my side telling me that I would be successful. Your sacrifices have not gone unnoticed and your unyielding love has kept me balanced.

To my children Kerry (Tamara) and Kanetha (Rontrell), thank you for staying the course, marrying the loves of your lives and bearing my beautiful grandchildren, Rhymes, Lyric, Kiznie and Ryithm; to my bonus children Ashley and Timothy II, thank you for loving me, even when you did not understand. It has meant more to me than you know.

To each of my nephews and nieces, I have always wanted my life to be an example for you. I am proud of your individuality, creativity, and love for our family. Continue to seek your truth.

To my God brother Corey and other true friends, I thank you for your support of Dr. J; no matter what turn my life has taken, you have pushed me and encouraged me to 'do me' – I love each of you. And finally, to my colleague and brother in the spirit, Dr. Walter Milton, thank you for sharing the vision of what could be.

# Foreword

There are fewer things harder in life to explain than what it means to be a Black woman. We often wax poetic about 'Black girl magic' and how 'Black girls rock.' And though, in theory, these beliefs are worthy of the women who proudly boast them, there is something less romantic brewing below the surface of us all. It is a truth so hard to speak that most of us walk the earth bound in chains of silence with links of shame, guilt and despair.

Historically, we, Black women, have always carried the weight of a world that hated us, yet craved us. From the days of slavery – when we had to endure the suffering of White men who lusted after and raped our bodies while their female counterparts despised our presence – to present day, when we are often maligned, unappreciated and abused by the very men we love and fiercely protect…oftentimes, men in our own families.

Through it all, we manage to keep our head(s) up. Thanks to a slogan we keep in our purse to whip out at a moment's notice, we know HE won't give us more than we can bear. The truth of the matter is, being a Black woman feels like heaven and hell had a baby. The women who share their stories in this book are a testament to that. The lyrics to the songs of our lives may be different, but the melody is the same.

We are born, we are hurt…we quietly march on. (I should put that on a fucking t-shirt, lol.) The point is, this book is the story of us…all Black women. It is the story of how we fight to be loved, we fight to be appreciated, we fight to be seen, we fight to be heard, we fight to not be hurt, and we fight to be valued.

The common denominator is that we are fighters. Even at our most peaceful state, we know a fight is always on the horizon. So, we stay ready, which is likely why we're often called "angry" – such a petty, misplaced generalization that does not nearly encapsulate all that we are.

Reading these stories will show you just how misused that adjective is. It will also show you how connected in spirit and experience we are, providing the utmost clarity of what it feels like to be a Black woman.

I am a Black woman…no longer silent.

*Jasmine Sanders*

# Contents

# Prologue

When I think about the plight of women, particularly Black women, as they matriculate through life, I think of my biological sisters and the millions of other women who share my hue. I am bombarded by numerous thoughts about this battlefield that we have so elegantly entitled, 'the world.' I say this because life, for many of our women, is akin to a war – daily wars on their minds, souls, spirits and yes, even their bodies.

Too many Black women and Black men find themselves in a mad race against time. Unfortunately, right when we think we are progressing, we realize that we are experiencing the "treadmill effect," going through the motions of swift movement, but not going anywhere (never arriving at 'some place') because we are strapped by the psychological chains of slavery. We are contending with things that we cannot even articulate because we are constantly fighting forces that were systemically placed to keep us neutralized. Being limited by the psychosis of psychological slavery fosters an environment for internalized racism, self-destruction, self-degradation, intrinsic aggression and self-hate (Black on Black destruction). These issues will linger, dwell, and eventually, find a home.

John Henrik Clarke, educator, historian, writer, scholar, lecturer, researcher and one of the greatest men who ever lived once said that, "We are a nation, within a nation, looking for a nationality." I would often say that we are victims of forced amnesia. Dr. Clarke clearly stated, "More critically, why do so many of us have a God-Concept assigned to us by other people. No people can be whole without an understanding [and defining] of their history?" Dr. Clarke concludes with the following:

*To me history is the clock that people use to tell their political and cultural time of day. It is also a clock that they use to find themselves on the map of human geography. The role of history in the final analysis is to tell a people where they have been and what they have been, where they are and what they are. Most importantly, the role of history is to tell a people where they still must go and what they still must be. To me the relationship of a people to their history is the same as the relationship of a child to its mother.*

Dr. Clarke got it right. I believe that there is a direct correlation with one knowing *self* from a historical context and their ability to see this grandiose experience we call life through its proper lenses. This increases one's probability of living a peaceful life – a life that is prosperous, purposeful, and beneficial to the larger human family.

If our young Black girls, who will eventually become Black women, find out who they are and where they come from and the many Godly contributions their people made to civilization, then they will excel even more in every aspect of their lives. They are the decedents of the movers and shakers of the universe. Women and men of African descent did not arrive on the scene from a monolithic ancestry but, an ancestry of variety, colorfulness, beauty, strength, brotherly and sisterly love, self-consciousness, richness, perseverance, queen-ship, king-ship, integrity, honesty, righteousness, respect for self and others, strength, wholeness, intelligence, brilliance, responsibility, and a commitment to family. We are recipients of a very painful, distinguished, diverse, and victorious culture and history. By nature, we are a collective people despite our unique differences.

As an educator, I have been blessed with the opportunity to work with educators, parents and students throughout the country and I am often amazed to see how schools are ill-equipped to work with Black female and male students. This often results in a major disconnectedness between Black female and male students and many of the people who are responsible for educating them. I must say that in many cases, it has nothing to do with an educator's lack of caring or intentions, but everything to do with ineffective approaches to educating these particular students.

I remember vividly talking to students in a particular school district about the quality of their education and the experiences they were having. A student made a poignant statement, "In school, we learn so much about other cultures, particularly, whites, [and] if you're not careful, you would think they invented air." She continued by asking, simple, yet profound questions, "What happened to us before we got on the boats against our will to come here? Who were we and how did we live and exist?" The answers to questions such as this guide the essays that are collected in this book.

To me, the existence of the Black woman is a conversation that must be held on sacred ground; because, it is a territory that we are all quite familiar with – the power, beauty, pain, love, selflessness, hurt, courage, healing, history of struggle, degradation and accomplishments, while being viewed in a world that devalues the endless contributions made, all encompasses her. The Black woman has withstood the test of time. She has an ever-evolving plight that shows significance to this world; grace with intellect, beauty and the elegance that God injected into her soul, which continues to shine, despite the conditions that come with the seasons of life. To know her is to love her, to need her and to realize her strength.

The co-author of this book, Dr. Jewell Winn, an accomplished educator currently serving as a higher education administrator, and I are dedicated to creating a resource for parents, students and community members. Our work in urban environments or environments populated with African American female students has propelled us to join in the pursuit to write this book.

Through our long and intense conversations regarding Black women and the current state of affairs pertaining to the plight of Black women, we decided to have a meeting of the minds and co-author what we believe to be a necessary read for all people concerned about our women.

Although, we both are individuals who care about all women in general, we decided to particularly focus on Black women. Dr. Winn and I have well over fifty years of service in the field of education. Those years have been laboriously dedicated to making a positive and lasting impact in the lives of others. This book is not only comprised of testimonials from

Black women, but it is a book of heartfelt, powerful and eye opening accounts of their life experiences. It is our firm belief that readers will find our book meaningful and helpful in their fight to combat the numerous and varied challenges that impact Black women.

Lastly, it is my hope and desire that our women become equipped with an artillery of excellence, weapons of knowledge/information that will help them navigate through, if not avoid many of life's road blocks. I pray the metaphoric roads my sisters have traveled serve as testimonies that our ancestors will rejoice and marvel over, providing a unique and thought-provoking perspective that serves as a most sacred and necessary discussion about and amongst people who are deeply concerned about and committed to the liberation of Black women.

*Dr. Walter Milton, Jr.*

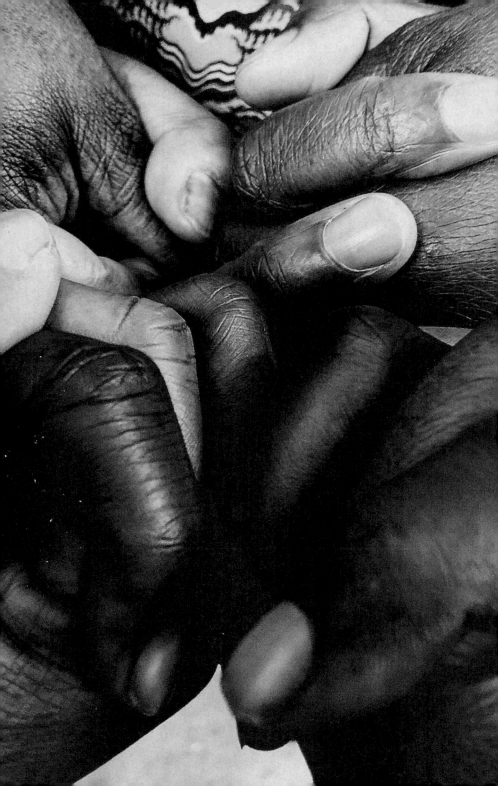

# Chapter One

## The Truth Must Be Told –
## How Does It Feel To Be A Black Woman?

*"Sometimes, I feel discriminated against, but it does not make me angry. It merely astonishes me. How can any deny themselves the pleasure of my company? It's beyond me."*
*– Zora Neale Hurston*

### Dr. Walter Milton, Jr.

Sometimes in life we have those defining moments; often there are a set of circumstances or events that drive us to the point of introspection. I remember talking about the storms of life and how they prepare us for brighter and clearer days. We are either entering a storm, in the midst of a storm or exiting a storm, nevertheless, there are monumental lessons gained in this process of life if managed properly. Growth is the ultimate outcome, especially when we embrace it and allow it to help us matriculate in an ever – changing world. I have grown significantly in my life by becoming observant, cognizant and sensitive to the plight of Black women. This has not only caused me to listen to what they do, but to watch what they say. Women in general have been blessed with an intuitive navigational system that can serve as a compass, especially when they are centered, righteous and healed from the brokenness of unfavorable dispositions, which they may have found themselves.

I have learned through relationships, some failed, some quite successful, having biological sisters and sisters that I gained along the way. However, I am still learning the value of taking responsibility for injuries that

I may have caused, because I understand that they may have been driven by things outside of myself. I am in the process of looking in the mirror of my life and asking difficult questions, such as what contributions have I made that caused pain, that confused, that helped/healed or that guided appropriately; am I a positive example of a good brother, lover, husband, father, friend, protector or provider; am I whole and complete; am I a good example to younger brothers, even my own children; do my actions, thoughts and deeds serve the Black Women of my life or those to whom I come in contact with properly?

One of the critical discussions that will be addressed in this book is that of Black male/Black female relationships. As one can attest, our relationships have been stained for many reasons, mainly, because of a painful past that still haunts us today and it requires us to assess our own psychosis and to admit to the haunting brutal reality of post traumatic stress disorder and the impact that slavery still has on our existence. Although, we have been conditioned to mitigate, forget and make excuses, it still remains and lodges itself on our doorsteps.

When I think of the conditions impacting Black people, I am reminded that the world is changing vastly. We are losing ground and do not realize that we are losing ground, however, simultaneously, we are gaining ground and do not know how to consolidate it. Some of us seem to have lost the art and drive to understand who we are, and what is our role in an ever-changing world.

We have to understand that we cannot imitate or be another people and rescue ourselves. We have to understand what happened to us, and the process used by those who have been in power and their ability to control images and information. They have marvelously created their depiction of the standard of beauty. Often times it contradicts the true image of beauty, that being said – the Black woman is BEAUTIFUL. However, the most successful thing and the most tragic thing, the one's who deceived the world, along with their point of view, is that they colonized the image of God. They started us on a tragic journey that many of us worship everything white, from a white God to white bread.

For many of us, we have a picture cemented in our mind. We worship a white Jesus over the weekend and plead to a white boss for economic survival the rest of the week and wonder why we lack respect for our Black women as well as Black men. According to John Henrik Clark, "If we changed the images around us to show ourselves in power, then we would not allow ourselves to be hostage in someone else's description. We cannot allow ourselves to be transformed and trapped into someone's cultural container, while reacting to being away from the culture that produced us. Sometimes we have to look back to move ahead."

We have to create healing devices so that we can establish healthy loving relationships that will see families as the cornerstones of our culture and nation, while recognizing that we are God Yahweh's people – this has to be manifested in all that we do and say. This is why we decided to take a deep dive in this powerful topic "The Truth Must Be Told – How Does It Feel To Be a Black Woman." I can proudly say, let the healing begin with me!

I encourage you to put your seat belts on. This body of writings is going to take you on an intense journey; you are going to read and listen to the souls of the collective list of Black women who have participated in this anthology. Their narratives are raw, painfully honest, humorous, and insightful; they address sexuality, love, both lost and gained, fatherlessness, the power of strong mothers and fathers; and they provide a litany of metaphors. These women are dealing with topics head on; they are not hiding behind their titles, status or made up superficial walls that we so often retreat to and live behind.

Their stories are indicative of scores of Black women across the United States in particular and the World as a whole. They herald from Los Angeles, California, Raleigh/Durham, North Carolina, Nashville, Tennessee, Washington DC, New York City, Dallas, Texas, Cleveland, Ohio, Detroit, Michigan, New Orleans, Louisiana, St. Louis, Missouri and other major cities and small towns throughout the nation. Although their geographical areas and settings may differ, their perspectives and insights can be quite nutritional to others. This book not only offers experiences and challenges, it offers applicable solutions.

My Mother, like most mothers was a gift from The Most High. The rhythm of her life spoke volumes, and she was the melodic sound that brought healing, peace and love to places and people that she touched. She was my Angel, the manifestation of many blessings. She, being the sole reasons that I love, respect, believe in and admire the strength in all women, particularly the Black woman.

So here I am, no option but to deal with the aftermath of all that was stored in my spirit embodied by the "Most High," my father and the other loved ones whom transitioned and joined the long list of ancestral forces beyond what we can see. Their dreams, hopes and aspirations still remain in those that carry their love and memories.

After writing three books, all related to the field of education, one might ask the critical question, why did you participate in writing a book highlighting Black women? My response could be one where I just shrug my shoulders and simply say, "I do not know." Instead I am compelled to say, why not? Actually, this is one of the most critical topics during this time of my life. I have had a front row seat in an amazing theater, watching the big screen of the Black women in my life; often the backdrop of strength is colored with metaphors of complexities left for one to sift through the pain of broken promises and stain of birthing a nation singly, while left carrying the bag alone.

This is a bitter reality; I have seen my mother fight through love, joy and pain of raising eight children – six all alone prior to meeting my father. I will always commend my father for being a father to children, while not the father of them. In many cases in Black America, many fathers leave the seeds that they plant to mothers to go it alone. My father exemplified the power and the beauty of what I call a Man's Man.

Getting back to the topic at hand, Black women exemplify this amazing gratefulness, which only they possess, and definitely, they deserve the right to be loved cherished and desired, because they are the greatest creation of the Most High God. As I matriculate through life, I discover scores of Black women who have been scorched by unfavorable relationships, single motherhood, poverty, single womanhood, rape, discrimination, sexism, while dealing with being marred by a history that is fraught with inaccuracies and untruths. However, the purpose of this book is to bring light and love to a group who has been pivotal to this world since the beginning of time.

This idea, to write about the so-called Black woman came from an experience that pierced my soul. The summer of 2016 my company, From The Heart International Educational Service, hosted a retreat for my staff in Nashville, Tennessee. I was training my staff and I had them to participate in a fish bowl activity. I categorized the teams by race and gender. One of the groups that I had organized was the Black woman in the company. I had a series of questions but I could not get past the first question when it came to the Black women.

The question was, "How does it feel to be a Black woman?" I had no idea that this question would invoke so much emotion. It was quite compelling; to say the least, this was a brutal reminder that Black women have absorbed so much and to their defense, they needed a mechanism to release. Hopefully, this book can serve as an instrument of release where, women, particularly Black women the world over can find themselves, somewhere in the pages of this book.

# Chapter Two

My stuff ain't like your stuff and your stuff ain't like my stuff – is it?

*"Focus on where you want to go, not on what you fear." – Anthony Robbins*

## Dr. Jewell Winn

My feelings about being a Black woman have changed numerous times over the course of my life. When I turned 50 years old a few years ago, I came to the conclusion that I was going to say what I felt, when I wanted to say it, and it didn't really matter who listened or who believed me. I went through a plethora of emotions—dang it, I had lived a half a century! There was nothing that could stop me from speaking what I felt was the truth as I knew it. I realized that my story could be told in ways that would relate to many women who look like me. In some instances, I felt ashamed of who I had been and then I began to feel very proud of whom I had become.

However, when we decided to collaborate on a book that would provide a space for women everywhere to share their story, I became excited but also afraid. How honest are we truly ready to be? Do we really know who we are? Would our stories change the opinion of what others think or have thought of us? Totally contrary to how I felt when I turned 50! Nevertheless, it is time. Too many of us suffer in silence. We are so inundated with taking care of everybody else except 'us'. We take on the hurt and pain of our friends, sisters, cousins, aunts, etc. We internalize those feelings—yes we do. We try to fix everything and everybody…except us. We get with our sister friends and talk about 'stuff'—how we are not going to take his $%*% no more or her #$*& no more and we give that same advice to each other, knowing all too well that we WILL take it because we are loving, forgiving, nurturing creatures that the Almighty made for his purpose. But—there is always a but; we all have a breaking point or a turning point I should say.

Stuff gets hard and I will continue to refer to situations as 'stuff ' because that is the easiest way to describe it. Decisions about relationships, that perfect career, weight loss/weight gain, children, parents, the car we want to drive, how to decorate our homes, must I mention our HAIR – weave or no weave, natural, color, braids, locks, and on and on. Now add hormones on top of all of that and the 'stuff' gets really hard. So how do we feel?

Now on to the deep stuff...real stuff like—being beat by your husband for breakfast, lunch and dinner and then forced to have sex with him, molested by a relative and sworn to secrecy your entire life, watch your best friend shoot up dope all night and all she wants you to do is make sure she doesn't overdose, your other best friend confides in you that she is bi-sexual and she has been in love with you for years, or you fall for a married man that tells you his wife is going to die and he wants you to be in his life when she's gone only to find out that she is in perfect health. Some might say that's just stuff you see on television, but those who have and are living it are too hurt and ashamed to talk about it. Then somebody asks you – how does it feel to be a Black woman? My question is, how do you THINK it feels to be a Black woman who has or is experiencing this 'stuff'?

Imagine waking up to the 'stuff' every day of your life but you have to put on your face and show the world that everything is okay because you are a strong Black woman and you simply cannot show your pain. Then again there are those who don't care. We get up every day and we don't put on our face; we are frowning – never smiling, we are snapping and cursing at anybody who steps in our way, we are yelling at the kids, we have road rage, we are on social media telling the world how pissed off we are about the smallest of things, we spend our last dime on a designer bag and can't put $5 in it because it makes us feel good, we get fly and go to the club hoping to find Mr. Right because Mr. Wrong has taken every ounce of self-respect and dignity from us, and the saga continues.

Now there is the flip side of the coin or that 'other' woman—the woman that is envied or hated on by many. That woman who has been fortunate enough to not experience a lot of pain and seems to really have it going on. She has been sheltered, spoiled, awarded, rewarded, accomplished, fed a silver spoon—life is good, right? She works hard, pays her own way through life, and has a great education, the perfect career, a good man, and successful children. So how does she feel to be a Black woman? We might be surprised.

So as you read this anthology, I hope that your spirit will be touched; that you will see value in the valley, that you will understand the battlefield of the mind, that you will lean in and not lean back, that you won't desire to be like Mary Jane but be all you can be. And lastly, understand as Steve Harvey stated, "Faith doesn't make it easy, faith makes it possible." Do not just change what you do – change what you believe.

# Chapter Three

The Quest To Be Loved –
It Is More Than An Emotion

*"In every crisis there is a message. Crises are nature's way of forcing change –
breaking down old structures, shaking loose negative habits so that something new
and better can take their place." – Susan L. Taylor*

**Norma Hedgepeth**

The question is asked – how does it feel to be a Black woman?  To be a Black
woman means I want to be loved, but I am afraid of being hurt; I deserve to
be loved, but I'm not; that I am capable of loving but I want it reciprocated.

I became a single mother at the age of 24. I had received my
bachelor's degree, moved back home and was working in a sewing factory
when I became pregnant. I had not found a job in my major and my parents
instilled in me at a very young age a strong work ethic. They didn't care
where I worked as long as I worked. It's nothing wrong with an "honest days
work – it could be in a pie shop," they would say. "If you don't work, you
don't eat."

My parents became pregnant, quit school, and married at ages16
and 17 to raise their family of six children. My mother later received her
GED and desired to continue her education however, the opportunity did not
avail itself.  My parents took over my mother's parents' farm when her father
had a stroke and was unable to work. Farming became their livelihood, in
addition to both working public jobs to provide for their family and make
ends meet. My mother was an awesome seamstress and made our clothes.

Growing up, my parents never relied on public service agencies for support. We were a tight knit family, visited mainly family members and kept our affairs pretty tight within the walls of our home. They were great providers and operated a tight ship with discipline and hard work.

They believed in "spare the rod, spoil the child," needless to say we knew who the parents were in the household. It reminds me of the slave owner's mentality, to whip us until we conformed. She would "whoop" us until we cried and then continued until we stopped. When my mother did not discipline us physically, she would lay some ole cliché's on us, like, "Ok ole girl, the higher you fly, the harder you'll fall" or "A hard head will make a soft behind." I would sometimes wonder – what is she talking about? It came into fruition exactly the meaning of the clichés she used as I grew older and experienced life.

My parents rarely showed affection in our presence; never heard them express publicly that they loved each other. Matter of fact, I can't remember them ever telling my siblings and I those powerful three words – "I love you," until my early 20's. I know they did, but it was implied. They made sure we had a roof over our heads, clothes on our backs and shoes on our feet. They were great providers. My father never talked to his girls about the type of men to select or expectations and characteristics to look for in a man.

The only thing I can remember the few times I dated as a teen, was when I was asked, "Can I trust you?" Surely I responded, yes. Deep inside I knew my mother was asking, "Can I trust you *not* to have sex?" We could take company or date at home at age 15 and a half, except for my oldest sister, on Sundays and then at age 16 on Wednesdays, however, at 9:00 p.m., he had to go, just like clockwork.

Growing up I was not provided with the necessary skills to develop positive healthy relationships in my life. I was ridiculed and criticized about boys I chose to date or chose not to date. My punishment was verbal, physical or material items taken away when I didn't conform. It became a continuous cycle until I became impervious to the material items being taken, the verbal humiliation, school activities withdrawn, and the whippings. I became a rebellious child and withdrawn; little did I know other teen girls were experiencing some of the same type of behaviors at home.

While in high school, my parents allowed me to obtain a part time job, after that I asked for very little. That gave me an outlet, especially after my mom banned my boyfriend from the house. I slipped to see my boyfriend when I wanted and had sex with him when I wanted. I graduated from high school and attended East Carolina University in Greenville, NC.

My mother detested the young man I considered my boyfriend, so he and I eventually broke up the first year of college. After that, I met this young man whom I believed cared for me. I was beaten so emotionally, I could never convince myself to commit to him, fearing that I would make the wrong choice or fearing someone could actually love me. I remembered him coming to my dorm room before leaving for his summer band camp to ask me to commit to a relationship. Oh wow, I remember vividly, where we were standing, the weather, people around, and what we were wearing. I was uncertain, I wanted to but I was afraid, I couldn't, so I didn't.

After receiving my bachelor's degree, I returned home to a place I said I would never, but I had lost my childhood – the very essence of who I was, or person I could have been – the love I missed out on had things been different. I so desired to recapture that part of my life if possible. I wanted the love from my parents, and to be accepted by both, especially my mother.

I started to work in a factory and began dating a man, who is my first son's father. Making minimum wage, no insurance and single, I sought out public assistance to assure I was taken care of. It was a temporary lifestyle but one well required. I wasn't sure if my baby's daddy would take on the responsibility of taking care of his child...but I knew for sure he had no intentions of taking us in marriage. Needless to say, he ran, leaving me to defend for our baby boy. Willie has only seen his son twice since he was an infant.

Being left to raise a child alone, I had flashbacks to my teen-age years of emotional distress, rejection, humiliation, loneliness, and the punishments. I promised myself, I would only depend on myself and to push forward in spite of my failures. I developed the attitude that I could take care of my child and me, I could be the mother and the father and I could raise my son to be a man. From that point, I did not look for a man who could take care of me; who would commit to me, or who would love me like I genuinely wanted to be loved. Maybe I felt undeserving, that a true relationship was unattainable or felt I just did not need a man. I built walls up so high and thick that Hercules could not tear down. I did not want to be hurt again; I never wanted to love again, because love is not supposed to hurt.

Ten years later, I became pregnant with my second child, another son. I loved this man with all my heart. He stayed around and supported me throughout my pregnancy and after my son was born. He was in and out of my life for years, not always as a couple but he was present. Suddenly, he was gone, married, started a new family in a new location. Visits became scarce but not extinct. It was an instant replay, different man, different child, and different circumstances, unfortunately, the same results. He was gone and once again I felt humiliated, lonely and unloved.

As I think back, my upbringing truly shaped my life. I love my parents for instilling in me strong work ethics, morals, values, the willingness to love, and the urgency to be responsible.

I realized years ago, that my parents reared me to the best of their ability and every action was a reaction of their rearing and experience. They were children raising children and their life lessons were based on the things they learned from their parents – to become providers, to have positive morals and values, and to be respectful.

They were married and stayed married and they dealt with hardships as they came and went. There were not any programs when they came along on effective parenting and marital skills; it was hands-on training – in other words, they had no blueprint. It wasn't always what they said but what they did. It was up to me, as I progressed into adulthood to build on the foundation they provided me. I can honestly say, my parents loved me and my mother still loves me.

I never blame others without evaluating myself; the responsibility does not lie on just one person or entity. I forgive too easily, but should never forget. I believe in giving each person a fair chance to prove him or herself. I have a big heart and most of the time it is broken. Someone recently asked me... "Why should I forgive my enemy only to be hurt again?" It was food for thought, and it is possibly my weakness.

Throughout my life, I always wanted to be a trendsetter and thought I had the intrinsic ability to do so. I wanted to do things differently than my other siblings. For the most part, I did, however it didn't come without consequences. I think my mother didn't know what to do with me sometimes. I was the first of my parents' children to have children out of wedlock, to graduate from college and to receive a Master's Degree, to join a sorority, the best, Delta Sigma Theta Sorority, Incorporated (Oooop, Oop!).

The "hard knocks" of life prepared me to be the Black woman I am today, to continue to depend on me ONLY – it is my safe haven. I think it helps me to accept disappointments or not have high expectations for others, sadly to say. It seems that the men or people I loved the most, hurt me the most. As I look deep into my inner soul, I desire the love of a Black man, and to be in a loving, healthy relationship. As some women would deny, there is no better place I would rather be than in the arms of a Black man, to feel his heart beat in rhythm with mine, and to be loved.

I truly believe that many Black families are so consumed with taking care of their families and working several jobs to make ends meet that they either lack the skills or lack the time to exemplify the real power of love to their child or children. Parents spoil their child/ren, but do they provide them with the necessary knowledge, exposure and skill set to help them navigate through life successfully? When I came along, my parents made sure I understood; I must work.

I believe that it is essential for Black men to be involved in their children's life – male and female. I have learned I can take care of the Black male, I can nurture him and love him, but I cannot raise a black male to be a black man. As a Black single mother with absent fathers, I needed to do what I knew best, to take care of my sons. I could not take chances where my sons were concerned. They were already considered a statistic at birth – being at risk for poverty, criminal activity, and incarceration – uneducated and less likely to succeed in life.

As parents, we need to give our children a great foundation to become responsible adults and citizens. We should love our children and esteem them. We should instill values and morals for them to live by. Teach them to never allow anyone to put shackles on their feet and to never become dependent on anything or anyone. Most importantly, never FEAR but to believe in YOURSELF, no matter the obstacle. Teach your child that they are privileged and deserve the best this world has to offer. It is important to teach your child, male and female how to love another person, how to treat that person and to find someone who they can spend their life with. Instill in your child characteristics to look for in a woman or man. Everyone deserves to have someone in their life to share things with, to raise a family with and to grow old together. Lastly, tell your child these three magical words, "I love you."

# Chapter Four

Seen but Invisible: Working While Black (WWB)

*"It's not the load that breaks you down, it's the way you carry it."* – *Lena Horne*

## Lola Johnson

Prejudices, invisible, underpaid, unvalued, "house niggas," affirmative action, inequality, lynching, rape, angry, unqualified, judged, incompetent, despised, colored, illiterate, dumb, untrained, uncivilized, bondage, thug, violent, irrational are few of the many words associated with the thoughts of White America about the Black population. I am a beautiful, inspiring, and intelligent Black woman. I love my "Blackness" and would not change it for any other race on this earth. I am strong and unbreakable and I can endure the prejudices of the "White American."

I have a bachelor's degree in accounting from Shaw University and a MBA in Finance from Strayer University. I have worked Credit and Collections for over 20 years. The first company I was employed with was Medical Device Manufacturing Company. I was responsible for collections, releasing orders, accounts receivable and credit evaluation. I started this company as a "temp" and worked myself into permanent employment within six months. Initially, I thought this was a great company to work for especially for a young woman just starting out. In my department there were approximately six Blacks, comprised of two males and four females, which was pretty well diversified. However, there were no Blacks in management. They offered standard benefits, sick and vacation leave, college re-imbursement, and 401-K.

Everything was progressing along with satisfaction until the second year. That's when my manager revealed his true colors as "white as snow." Until then my White male Manager and I had a decent working relationship. "Mr. X," my manager was about 50 years old, with 20 years of experience in Finance. Because he had been in the workplace for many years of course, he was a " know it all," a connoisseur in the profession, he thought. I admired him for his expertise and thought I could learn from him and grow in the company. But this one particular day changed my entire outlook and respect for him.

My job entailed me to contact customers to determine why their account was delinquent and to set up a payment schedule, resolve disputes such as pricing issues and shortages. Each collector was given a portfolio of customers to work with. I was working with a customer, a valued and loyal customer who had become delinquent in their payment. Through a great deal of communication with the customer, we settled on a payment plan while continuing to supply them with their regular orders. I always had a great rapport with my customers and delivered effective customer service.

Once everything was settled, I met with my manager and shared the results. He disagreed with my decision. He was FURIOUS. His face became flushed. His eyes blazed with anger as he began flailing his hands around. He ordered all shipping be discontinued. I argued my points, but he denied any further shipments until the account became current. He was the boss and he made the final decision. I followed up with a courtesy call to inform the customer that his credit had been denied until his account became current.

Later that day, my manager came in to the cubical section where I worked with co-workers and asked, "Lola did you contact the customer? I responded, "Yes." Then he responded, "That's good because you were acting like a real 'B.' He made this comment in the midst of my co-workers. I turned around, looked at him in astonishment; my co-workers were amazed that the manager referred to me as a "B." And my follow up response was, " I know you must be calling me BEAUTIFUL, because I know you're not calling me a BITCH." He followed with a laugh of sarcasm, and said, "that is right, that would be the right thing to say." He turned and walked back into his office.

I was dismayed at his comment and behavior. I became quite pissed and humiliated. I have always felt that White men classified Black women as bitches and it made me reflect back to slavery when they, the White slave owners raped the Black woman and used their bodies for their own sexual deviances and pleasures. It made me think about the White wives becoming jealous and insecure and demanded that the Black woman was beaten.

So many thoughts ran through my mind; my manager had given me a job to perform but I was not given any autonomy to make a business decision. My manager's response reflected on the behavior and attitude White men always had towards the Black woman. It infuriated me. From that day forward, I only consulted with him when necessary. I was a young Black woman at this time, had just moved from home and felt I needed to prove myself. I was working on my bachelor's degree and the company was reimbursing me for my education, so I felt the need to keep my mouth shut. In fact, while working at this company I received my MBA degree in Finance. I knew there was an end to this madness, while they used me; I used them to meet some of my goals. I told myself sit still, your day will come.

Within my seven - year tenure, I continued servicing my customers professionally, within the guidelines of the company policies. My dealings with him was on an as need basis, only when necessary.

A supervisory position finally opened up in the collections department. I talked to my manager about it and he encouraged me to apply. At that time I had obtained my bachelors and working on my MBA. He interviewed me and I thought it went well but later to find out he had promised the job to a White woman who was a temporary employee and who had no credit and collection experience. In actuality, I felt he was intimidated by me, as a Black strong, intelligent opinionated woman who he knew was qualified for the position. During my time there, I received several bonuses based on my performance or financial goals that were set by the company.

After being turned down, I felt the need to contact Human Resources and the result was nothing. I realized that I was in a dead end job.

I was miserable, underpaid, and invaluable. I watched as others were hired and promoted to positions based on the color of their skin – purely "racial favoritism." I stayed for three more years regretting every moment. I felt trapped and "black balled" for internal promotions and external employment.

Finally, I left this company and was hired at Lloyd Corporation as a Credit and Collections Specialist. I knew I needed to leave my present place of employment; I was relieved. I soon learned there were no Black managers at Lloyd Corporation and interns that were hired were all White, not one single Black intern came through the door. In one year, eight Black women resigned from this company ranging from HR to the legal department. There was an incident that the corporation paid out a lawsuit because a White employee tied a noose and placed it on a Black male employee's desk. With all their power, it was revealed.

I do not fear White people but quickly I realized that I was up the creek without a paddle. The employees were not cordial, they would not speak and I quickly reminded myself that I was not there to gain friends but to perform a task and go home. Also I realized, I was experiencing "being Black while working" (BWW) in the White man's world (WMW). I told myself I must be invisible because I would walk behind a White person or pass them in the hallway and they would speak to their White counterparts while sealing their lips as if my "Blackness" would rub off on them.

I continued to remind myself that I could handle this and no one would push me away. My compensation was decent and I accepted working in the White man's world. Life right now was okay. After a year, I applied for a financial analyst position and, of course, I was not recommended for it. Not long after that my male supervisor quit and was replaced by a White female. Things changed.

Three months, after my manager's arrival, yearly reviews, were upon me. We met and she reviewed my evaluation and I was shocked. She made false accusations that threatened my livelihood. She accused me of threatening a White female employee via email, abusing time, arriving to work and returning from lunch late. She literally said I was a "THIEF of [company] time." In one instance, I asked to take sick time and she responded, "If you are sick, maybe you should take a leave of absence until your health improves."

She stated I was "ill-prepared" for meetings during account reviews and was unfamiliar with the status of my assigned accounts. In essence, I was illiterate and lacked knowledge in my job responsibilities, according to her. Of course, I disputed every accusation. How could she make those references to me and about me, when she didn't fully understand my responsibilities?

Let me explain. During meetings, I would refer back to the notes on my computer to ensure I was providing accurate information concerning my accounts. In the note section, we are given a certain number of character spaces, so I created acronyms that a credit and collections specialist would know, but being she did not have knowledge in this area, she had difficulty understanding the language. While I verbally explained to her, she added that I lacked effective communication skills and she wondered how well I communicated with my customers. She continued with insults, alluding that I lacked effective communication skills, written and oral.

Finally, she placed me on a personal improvement plan, where she would coach me in learning my job role and responsibilities and recommended that I receive an one percent raise increase. My task was to create the schedule and the areas of discussion, because she was unaware of my role and duties.

I followed up with Human Resources who took the side of management. HR asked me what I had done to make people retaliate against me, want to hurt me, as to say I was the culprit and deserved it. Basically, she said I was the villain. The drama is still alive at my place of employment. It is apparent, my manager would love for me to turn in my resignation. What she does not know is, she can ridicule me and make derogatory statements, however, I am a strong Black woman. I will stand my ground to the end. I will not leave until I decide to leave.

In corporate America, Black women are generally scorned. We are often labeled as being angry, incompetent, lazy and deficient. White men usually hire and promote the ones that are closest to his image and would rather mentor the White man or woman than any other race. I am appalled by the fact that Black America is as capable as the White man but we have to think and work harder and behave according to their guidelines and practices to work in their world.

I find that racism is very much alive and well, subtle or blatantly in your face. Martin Luther King died fighting for equality for the Black race and I often feel we have not progressed too far from where he left us. Sure, we have had a Black President to serve for eight years, but now Trump is in. I ask myself, is there any hope? Working While Black in White Corporate America. I digress.

# Reflections from the Soul

---
---
---
---
---
---
---
---
---
---
---
---
---
---
---
---
---
---

# Chapter Five

Climbing The Mountain of Perceived Insurmountable Odds

*"Whatever is bringing you down, get rid of it. Because you'll find that when you're free . . .
your true self comes out."* — *Tina Turner*

### Candace Omar

As I sit on the sofa listening to the rainfall, the leaves rustling back and forth,
it takes me back to a gloomy, dark place in my life. A time in my life that was
so dismal, a time I wish my hard drive would delete for eternity. But for that
to happen would mean I would lose some so-called happy moments in my
life; I need all that I have. My mother had moved her boyfriend in, shortly
after the separation of her third husband. This is a time that our family
became dysfunctional and changed my life forever.

My siblings and I often expressed to our mother that we didn't like
this man. He was verbally abusive to all of us – my mother and her children
– and disrespected what we thought was our home. He moved in before the
scent of my father had disappeared and we were saddened by the sudden
change in our lives. We had lived a pretty decent life, prior to this catastrophe
my mother caused. My mother was an administrative assistant in a local law
firm and my stepfather an industrial engineer in a local manufacturing
business.

My stepfather loved us like his own; he was a provider and a family
man. We enjoyed family time; we shared meals and watched TV together,
laughed, played and had fun. We went to church, to the movies, enjoyed
bicycling and vacations. We did all the things that a family wanted and

needed. He was a good, wholesome man; he loved my mother and his children. My biological father no longer played an intricate part in my life, but this man was the only father I have ever known and loved, and he was taken away by bad choices my mother made and this so called man that brutally took his place.

Needless to say, changes were made instantly within our household, when this person moved in. Financially we were broke, my mother making a little over minimum wage was unable to provide for us. We digressed from a middle class family to poverty level. There were no longer luxurious meals on the table, no more entertainment and family outings, and vacations became obsolete.

According to Maslow, our basic survival needs were dimensioned, a digression most definitely had occurred; we weren't even on the chart. Emotionally we were broken, we could not trust our mother or this new man who had overpowered our home. There was constant turmoil among us because of all the uncertainties that had plagued our once happy family.

Struggles to maintain power and landlines, dealing with foreclosures, vehicle repossessions, and keeping food on the table became a way of life for us. My mother could no longer afford our 2-story suburb home, therefore, we moved into a two bedroom single mobile home in the country. My sisters and I slept in one full sized bed and my mother and her new love in another room with a twin bed. Our savings plummeted as quickly as a "drop zone" ride at an amusement park. Not a great feeling. We were in a state of emergency.

This new man in our lives was young and had no sense of responsibility for his new-found family. He used drugs, was unemployed and had no tolerance or respect for four young children. It was not uncommon to come home to find the house filled with the smell of marijuana, cocaine and alcohol bottles on the table. We hated him and all he stood for. He picked arguments with my mother and constantly demanded my mother to side with him, despite the situation. He would say, "the kids do not like me and they are turning you against me." He would antagonize my younger siblings by comparing himself with their biological father and often made comments that he was the "new sheriff" in town and "what once was, is no longer."

He called one of my sisters a lesbian, dike or butch and any other derogatory name he could think of, because she wore jeans and tennis shoes and kept some kind of ball in her hand. He would barge in the girls' room when he knew we were disrobed and pretend it was an accident. He made regular comments to me about my bodily changes that made me quite uncomfortable. He would tell my mother, that I was "screwing," and she needed to keep me under lock and key. He constantly compared my breast size to the size of my mothers. I became self-conscious around him. One day in passing, his hand swept across my behind, he looked at me and smiled and said, "I know you like it."

A feeling of embarrassment came over me, I felt nasty, and betrayed. This man was targeting me. I was a victim in my own home. I was being robbed – he was taking over my life, my body without my permission – he was like a "thief in the night."

It seems I could never get rid of him; when the family was together I was always in his direct sight. He would stare and make me feel uncomfortable. He always had a sly grin on his face. I hated him! This became a regular for him and the more I shared with my mother, the more she would say, "Y'all don't want me to be happy."

I vividly remember, such a gloomy day as it is today. I was about 14 years old. My mother had left to go shopping and she took my other three siblings with her. Just about the time I thought I would enjoy being at home alone, he came home. He was as drunk as a 'skunk', staggered to the table to suck up line after line of 'nose candy'. Sometimes it sounded as if he wouldn't catch his breath, he snorted so long and hard. I wished many times he would not – that he would stifle himself until every breath left his body and he would keel over. No such luck. The more he consumed, the more intense I became. I wondered how I could get out of this room and house without him knowing. I knew it was impossible because had I lifted a window, he would hear it and the front and back doors were closest to him than they were to me. I became stiffer than a corpse in a morgue, to keep him from realizing I was there. Finally, I moved and the lamp fell on the floor. He called out, "Who's back there?" My heart began to beat a 100 miles per hour; my legs became tense and my hands clinched in a fist. I was as afraid as the time I saw, the movie, "Halloween," back in the late 70's, when scary movies were actually scary. Then I heard him stumble over the kitchen chair. He crept across the floor, down the hallway. With each step, the boards cracked. Finally, there he stood, looking at me, standing in the corner.

He smiled, a very sly grin, one that brought on an eerie feeling all over my body. I vividly heard him saying, "This is what I have been waiting for." He grabbed at me, he fell on the bed, and I ran out of the room into the family room. He grabbed me again as I headed towards the door, pulled me back and pushed me on the sofa that was sitting near the window.

Outside there is a big oak tree, it was raining, the leaves were rustling back and forth from the wind, just like it is as I write this. He tore my blouse open and put his mouth over my breast and then thrust his tongue into my mouth, down my throat, while holding my arms over my head and pressing all his weight onto me to keep me from moving. Then he pulled his penis from his nasty, stinky jogging pants he wore, tore off my underwear and thrust his penis into me. He continued on and on each time harder and harder with all his power until he could not throb it any longer. Finally, he rolled over on the floor and he muttered, breathlessly, "You better not tell anyone, your mother, not anyone." I lay there; with tears rolling down my face, I was numb.

Suddenly, the leaves moving on the tree woke me from my comatose state. I turned my head and outside the window; I could hear the rain falling and the rustling of the leaves. That saved me, that day. I laid there – I couldn't move. I wondered to myself, "What did I do to deserve this? I felt deprived, humiliated, mutilated and robbed; I didn't know what to do.

After that I was a different person. I became very angry. I acted out in school, academically and socially. I was suspended several times for fighting; skipping classes and school. My grades suffered tremendously, although I did not fail, I did just enough to get by. I started to smoke cigarettes, marijuana and drink alcohol; everything was a go for me. I did not care anymore. Whatever happened just happened.

After a tremendous amount of reflection and healing, as well as intense counseling, I was able to start putting my life together. I relied heavily on my siblings and friends for moral support. I wouldn't have made it without them. I took anti-depressants on a daily basis to keep me balanced. I did what that "scumbag" asked me to—I never told my mother. Through the years, I blamed her, however, I forgave her. To hold on to hatred is like holding on to a hot iron, it will continue to burn you to the bone until there is nothing there.

Finally, I graduated from high school and enrolled into a local community college then transferred to a four year university and graduated with a BS Degree in criminal justice. Later, I pursued a degree in Law

To respond to the question, how does it feel to be a Black woman encompasses so many things? I was subjected to uncertainties, confusion, poverty, lies and betrayal, drug abuse, sexual abuse and rape, humiliation and neglect. Despite those awful years of my life, I flourished into a beautiful, confident and successful woman who can love, who can reflect on that devastating time in my life and not allow my past to determine my future. But I will never forget, the big ole oak tree, the rain and the rustling of the leaves that brought me back into reality that day that saved me.

# Chapter Six

Growing Up and Mastering
The Spirit of Perseverance

*"A crown, if it hurts us, is not worth wearing."*
*– Pearl Bailey*

## LaRhonda McLemore Cockrell

Back when I was growing up, I used to think the way we lived was a normal way of living life. We lived in Section 8 housing in Franklin, Tn. My sisters and I went to a predominately White elementary school. However, there was a period in my life where my mom found herself experiencing some hardship financially which led us to being homeless. At one point, we lived in our car. We went from living in my mom's car, a mission and family members house. When we lived with one of our family members, I was molested. I was so terrified by the incident that I buried the thoughts, emotions and feelings in the back of my head until I was an adult.

I later learned that the same thing that happened to me as a child happened to my mother when she was a child. In my opinion, when my mom decided to move to Nashville things began to shift for the worse. My mom became involved with multiple men. With more men came more children. With additional children left us with a void of our mom not being around. My mom was working multiple jobs in order to provide for us. After a while, my siblings and I learned to survive and take care of us. We helped each other get dressed in the morning for school, we made breakfast for each other and we made sure each other got to and from school safely. I believe that is where I learned the trait of being dependable, independent and also putting myself last. I knew my younger sisters needed me and I was there for them even if it meant I missed out on my childhood. Fast forward to high school, after living with multiple family members, I became really anxious to be in our own place and I would push my mom to find us a place to live. My mom was approved for a housing project on South 8th but she didn't want to live there. My mom may not have had the best job or the best car however where we lived was very important to her because she was accustomed to a certain way of living.

As mentioned before, my mom found herself at a very low point at that time her in life. My mom was so anxious to be in her own place that we moved immediately into the first place offered which was in the hood. My mom viewed the living situation as temporary so she didn't purchase furniture for the place. I remembered sleeping on blow-up mattresses, mattresses with no box springs and at one point I had a really thick carpet I would make a palette on at night. However, the place was so disgusting I remembered not taking showers there. I would take a bath in the sink. At night, you could hear the rats running back and forth over our sheets. I recall telling myself that night; I would never live like this again. Little did I know that in those earlier years of my life God was preparing and molding me for a much bigger assignment. He was teaching me humility and humbleness. I learned how to be motivated by circumstances. I learned then, that there is always a way to achieve what you need to achieve despite your circumstance.

Once I was old enough to get a job, I started working immediately but the only thing I didn't factor in was a car. At that time, my mom was very cruel when it came to giving me a ride back and forth to work. As a result, I would walk from East Nashville to Dickerson Road in the cold, snow and rain. If you're from Nashville, then you'll understand that that was a major walk. Let me explain just a little. I had to cross a major intersection at the age of 15 or 16 to get back and forth to work. I was determined. I believe in that moment of my life I learned self-determination. If I really wanted something done, I had to do it myself. I couldn't depend on anyone else to do it for me, not even my own my mother. Talk about learning independence at a very early age in life…. After working several dead end jobs, I was able to purchase my very first car with cash. I was the happiest girl on the planet but with a car there was the responsibility of a license, insurance, maintenance and gas. I had a car before I had valid driver's license. Consequently, I found myself with a lot of traffic violations and traffic school, lol (not the best idea). As I sit back and reflect now, I honestly didn't think that entire scenario through.

Fast-forward to senior year "05-06". One day after school, I was over a friend's house getting my hair done for senior pictures and I received the worst phone call of my life from my older brother. He called me to inform me that our father had passed away. Even today, I remember that day like it was yesterday. I was a daddy's girl. I'm not saying my father was a perfect man however he was perfect in my eyes. Later on in life my mom and I had a conversation about my father—years after he had passed away. My father was the one who introduced my mom to intravenous heroin. Intravenous heroin is where a person injects the heroin into their bloodstream with a needle. My father on the other hand, died from a cocaine overdose. I didn't quite understand how drug affects and how serious they were back then, but as an adult I do now. Drugs, alcohol and any other substance can easily destroy families.

A couple of months before graduation, I found myself seriously involved with an older guy. He was one of the biggest drug dealers in East Nashville. I recall this event in my life so vividly. I was in ballet with my friends and my instructor Ms. Gentry said, "Your hips are spreading. Are you sure you aren't pregnant." My best friend and I went home that evening to do homework and she pulled out some pregnancy tests. (Now, my best friend at the time was much more sexually active then I was. I had only had sex once, however (let the truth be told) it only takes one time.) She took a test and the results were negative. She then suggested I should take the pregnancy test and I said okay. I already knew it was going to come back negative, but I took the test anyhow and the result was POSITIVE.

I immediately began to sweat and panic. In my mind, I'm like this can't be right. Long story short—I was three weeks pregnant. I found myself pregnant a month before graduating high school. I was so disappointed in myself and I was so afraid to share the information with my mother. In fact, I didn't even share it with my dance teacher because just a week or so ago, she was helping me fill out applications for college. I knew that at that time I wasn't ready to have a kid. We were already struggling; I didn't see a future with the guy I was dating and I wanted to go to college. Under the circumstance, I went ahead and shared the information with my mom. After I shared the information with mom, she left the decision up to me at the age of 17. I decided not to have the child. As a result, the guy I was dating became verbally and physically abusive. In his mind he thought I was sleeping with someone else; it was someone else's child, and that's the reason I didn't decide to have it. I believe now, as an adult, I never really dealt with that situation and it lingered on throughout my life. Ultimately, it's played a part throughout other relationships during the course of my life.

Adulthood Phase 1 – I made it to college...I MADE IT TO COLLEGE! I believe that was the first step to my life moving from hell to heaven. I was in college. I had a nice car. I had a great job and I had my own place. I was so happy but I was soon reminded of where I came from. I was sitting in class, my very first quarter of school. It may have been the third or fourth week of school. I received a phone call from the Department of Human Services (DHS) that would forever change my life. The caseworker on the other line said, "Is this LaRhonda McLemore?" I said, "Yes, how can I help you?" She went on to say that my mom tested positive for cocaine and marijuana and if someone didn't come and get my siblings that they would be taken into State custody. I informed her I was on the way. That particular moment changed my life forever. A temporary situation turned into seven years. I was supposed to take temporary custody of my two siblings until my mom got herself together however that turned into seven years of custody of my two younger siblings. During those seven years, my younger sibling became pregnant with my nephew. She was only 14 when she had him.

Adulthood Phase 2 – Thinking back, I thank God that I didn't lose my mind and that I held on to His promises that He had for my life. In spite of all that had transpired, I was still able to graduate college and obtain my associates degree in fashion design and merchandise. I can't honestly say that there was one individual who made a huge impact on my life. What I will say is that it took a lot of self-encouragement, hard work, dedication and resilience to get through it. There were several individuals who helped me along the way—women and men. Eventually, I went back and obtained my bachelor's degree in Psychology. I am now currently working on my master's degree in Professional School Counseling. I plan on going ALL the way—you will call me Dr. McLemore one day.

Many individuals talk or share about the struggle but not many actually share or talk about how they were able to get through the struggle. The very first thing I had to get together was my mindset. There were a lot of negative seeds planted within me that could've grown into weeds. If I would've watered, nurtured and taken care of those negative weeds, there is no telling where I would be today. A lot of people won't share this, but I will. I had to pay attention to what others were trying to plant in my head and within me because I had to live with the harvest. I spent many years of detoxing myself from the waste that was planted within. I had men tell me I would never amount to nothing. I was told I was ugly – no one would ever love me or want to marry me. My mom didn't validate my siblings and I. She never told us we were pretty or that we were worth it. Let me tell you—I know that I am WORTH IT! I am VALUED! God made me fearfully and wonderfully.

We become what we think. Our thoughts manifest into the reality of our lives. So, if you think it, you become it. Before you learn a new way to be, you must first learn a new way to think. It may seem hard at first, however after you start doing something daily it becomes a part of your routine. I wrote down scriptures, positive affirmations about myself, and quotes that made me feel inspired. I would literally place them everywhere in my apartment and car. I would even make them screen savers on my phone. It's a daily reminder that everything is going to be okay and that you are WORTH IT!

I stay PRAYED UP. I can't say this enough. Once I became elevated, I began to experience the devil's wrath. If he can't attack you at work, he will attack you at school. If he can't attack you through your friends, he will attack you through your boyfriend or husband. He will use your family and sometimes those attacks are the worse. It hurts when you love your family so much and sometimes you don't quite understand why they are attacking you in this way. However, I came to realize that it was not them it was the spirits within them. You are never fighting flesh. It's always a spiritual warfare. I had family members who may have been jealous or insecure with my success thus far because they never took that chance to pursue their own dreams. They would rather run up on me instead of towards their dreams and goals. Beloved, know this, those who want to see you fail already don't care for you regardless of how much they say they do. It's not my job to worry about getting their approval.

I am focused on doing me and keeping my eyes on the race set out before me. I am allowing my success to speak for me. I am moving in silence. I have figured out those people who disguise themselves as supporters but they really are denouncers— so I just removed myself from them and moved on happily with my life—that included some family members too. I will not be fooled anymore.

I had to find mentors and to be completely honest about my journey – I didn't get a mentor until I was an adult. The funny thing about it is that the majority of my mentors now say—you really don't need me. You have it all together. I believe you can run this business or sell this book without me. You are ready girl!! I've always felt a certain way when it came to selecting women to be mentors. A majority of them—not all, are wounded. I can wholeheartedly say I didn't receive a warm and cozy embrace from the majority of them as potential mentors initially. Let me tell you why. There are a lot of women who are successful but they are wounded. They are wounded by failed relationships, failed businesses, failed dreams and goals—the list could go on. But I learned from this. I decided to be more selective. As a result, I vowed to NEVER EVER be like some of the women I encountered in my past as a potential mentor.

I learned the importance of bouncing ideas off of others. I sought others in my field who were already doing what I wanted to do. And, I didn't come empty handed. I wanted others to share their wealth of knowledge with me, so I made sure I had something to offer in return. For instance, I wanted to learn about the non-profit/business world from this phenomenal woman by the name of Dr. Winn. In return, I offered her my expertise, which, at the time, was social media management. She needed the word out about her phenomenal new building, events and different activities that were taking place at her facility. As result, I learned some valuable information that I could take to my business while I also helped her with her current business. It's about being an asset versus a liability.

I am unapologetically ME! I don't waste my time trying to be anyone else but me. When I first entered this unknown world of business, college and the "in" crowd I was immediately reminded that I didn't really fit in. I was okay because I had already identified three very important things: 1. Who I was? 2. What I stood for? 3. What my insecurities were?. I define myself as being a woman first—a woman of God. I speak a lot about God and how he has helped me tremendously throughout my life. I sometimes receive a lot of backlash about me speaking about God but you have to remember I had already made it clear who I was. I am a child of the most high.

I now make it very clear what I stand for—I don't tolerate negative energy, excuses or negative people. I will shut it down immediately. I also stand for being unapologetically assertive and bold. This helped me when people began to start trying to criticize me or call me names. We all have insecurities but the key for me is that I own my space confidently. I am okay with being misunderstood – it happens.

I will leave you with this – don't be surprised when you are swarmed with a lot of people. Remember, bugs are drawn to the light too. I pray that my authenticity about my life, thoughts and experiences will bless your life in such an awesome way.

# Reflections from the Soul

# Chapter Seven

## "One Thing About Life – *Shift* Happens"

*"You may encounter many defeats, but you must not be defeated. In fact, it may be necessary to encounter the defeats, so you can know who you are, what you can rise from, how you can still come out of it."* – Maya Angelou

### Aretha Garr

How does it feel to be a Black woman? Being a much wiser, grateful, enduring, powerful, and self-sufficient Black woman…. I would never want to be anything else. For so many years starting from my earliest memories in childhood, it was not easy. Looking back, I know I have been blessed and graced with a very strong and powerful force, as a lesser woman would not have endured the many things that I have.  And, as a proud and fearless Black woman, I share my story with all of it's ugliness, darkness, and loathing to enlighten and empower another Sister feeling alone or undeserving of the trials and tribulations of life.

My stepfather told me once "if not you, who?". He said this to me because I believed I had endured all I could stand and I was tired of feeling like the burden was just too much for me. I wanted to give up. I will not run from the thoughts of suicide but I will not say I wholeheartedly was ready to end my life. I just wanted a little of the pressure taken off because all I knew was pressure. That pressure, that pain, that hurt, that relentless feeling of strife is why I am A PROUD BLACK WOMAN.

As a little girl growing up in Kentucky, I was never told I was pretty. I heard the word a lot but no one ever told me that I was. The words that I would hear were so negative, mean, cruel, and crippling that what I do remember is how they make me feel right now. I am 43 years old and it still stings.

I am a caramel brown African American woman who many have inquired whether or not I am from the Islands. I laugh. Me, from the Islands, no. Both of my parents are "Black" people from very small towns in Kentucky. What about me make you ask? I hear things such as your skin is clear, flawless, and your skin tone is beautiful.

I find it amusing, as none of that is true of me. My nickname when I was a little girl was skillet, Blackie, ugly, and etc. You get the picture. This was most of my life as a child, teenager, and most of my life in my twenties. The funny thing is (even now) I do not believe I am a beautiful woman. Why? No one ever told me when I needed it most. As a young girl being bullied relentlessly for not having nice clothes or shoes, for my hair not being combed and groomed, for not being light enough, for not being loud enough, and not being smart enough. It just seemed like nothing I did was "not enough".

Because of the treatment I received as a child, I did not have a lot of friends. My two best friends were Rosa and Jennifer. I would get on my bike and ride around the neighborhood that I had created into an imaginary city. Wherever I went Rosa and Jennifer were with me. We would have fun for hours. We would live in huge mansions and drive fancy cars (our bikes) and we were married to real handsome men and had great children.

If my friends, Rosa and Jennifer, and I weren't riding bikes, we were playing school. I was always the teacher and they would be two of my students in my large classroom.

The other things we loved to do was play house. I had a play kitchen set with a life-size Black doll. I would be the husband and one of my friends would be my wife. The doll would be our child.

The games I played with Rosa and Jennifer could go on for hours. My mom would always call my name from downstairs or the front door or at my bedroom door and say to me, "Aretha, are you ok? What'chu up there doing? I haven't seen you in a while."

I would always say, "Nothing mama." I am just playing. She would be satisfied and I would get back to playing.

I loved Rosa and Jennifer. They loved me. They never picked on me or made me feel bad. They never called me names or deliberately left me out of things they were doing. Anything and everything that I wanted to do, Rosa and Jennifer would do it. What made them so great was that they were imaginary. Due to being picked on so much, I made my own friends. With these two friends, I didn't need real ones.

If my imagination did not want Rosa and Jennifer, I would just go into my head. This is what I called it and would come up with the greatest stories in my head. These stories would be so profound that I would act them out with my dolls, thanks to the greatest man that ever lived, my father, Alvin Garr. I had so many dolls that I didn't know what not do with myself. I had all of the Charlie's Angels, Strawberry Shortcake, Glamour Gals, Barbie, Soni & Cher, Donnie & Marie, just to name a few.

My bedroom would be a city with so much going on that I would take naps in the middle of the floor from being tired with all of the drama going on in my head. Funny now, as I write this memoir, I was a pretty imaginative kid who was a loving, caring, and gracious child but, unfortunately, had no one to validate that for me, but my dad.

I will talk about him soon. Right now, I am just getting this out of my head because someone asked me to write my story, because it was interesting and worth sharing. Fortunately for me, I was blessed to have a great father and stepdad. Not many people can that say. What is even more rare is that they each loved me more than my mom.

I have memories of my mom before she became so self-centered and selfish where she would sit in the floor and play dolls with me. I remember she and I playing Hungry, Hungry Hippo in the middle of the living room floor. I remember us holding hands and walking through very tall grass down this path to the IGA where we lived. During this walk, we would reach railroad tracks and my mom would pick me up in order to cross over them because she didn't want me to hurt myself.

The housing projects that we lived in had a park. She would take me to the park so that I could play on the sliding board and merry go round. While I played on these things, she would sit on a bench or the curve to talk with some of the other women around.

I remember being really sick and my mom wrapped me up in this Fred Flintstone blanket to carry me to the local hospital. It was freezing cold outside. The hospital from the housing projects had to be 15 miles so imagine a slim, 5'5" woman carrying a seven year old. I only remember this because, my fever was so high I was sweating and shivering at the same time.

We didn't have a phone and I cannot remember why she had to walk as opposed to getting a ride. My mom carried me out the door and began walking. Through the blanket, I was shivering and she was crying and praying. *Please don't let anything happen to my baby. She is all I have.*

I remember that like it was yesterday. Why does that memory stick with me so heavily? Because this was my mom when she was her greatest – somewhere along the way, my mom was not like that anymore. I am not sure what happened but my mom stopped being that type of mother. She became selfish and self-centered. The only person that mattered to her was herself.

My mother never drank liquor, smoked cigarettes or drugs. What she loved more than herself was men. Many of these men she slept with for money. I know this for a fact as I witnessed most of her discretions. I saw things that I should not have and I know about things no child should know about their mother.

My father, Alvin Garr, was my biggest hero. I loved him so much that when I looked at him all I saw was greatness. I do not mean a superficial, cliché type of greatness because he was my father but because it was the little things my father did that my mother was supposed to.

My fondest memory of my dad was when he took me to Lexington, Kentucky to a store named Hill's. Hill's may be a hybrid of Wal-Mart and Target. It was me, my dad, and his girlfriend Bernice. I remember my dad wanted me to try on some shoes. My shoes were hideous. I do not even know the name of those shoes. I just know that they hurt my feet. I also knew I did not want to take them off in front of my dad.

I remember he wanted me to take them off and I wouldn't. I didn't want him to see. He always called me 'pumpkin' or 'miss lady'. I remember he looked at Bernice in frustration and she nodded at him. He said that he was going to go look at something but would be back. I sat on Bernice's lap and she talked to me. She eased my mind as she was taking my shoes off. I clinched my toes tightly as a way to say, I didn't want her to remove my shoes.

I didn't want my dad or Bernice to see my dirty, holey socks that were mixed match. One of my socks was a baseball sock with two blue stripes at the top and the other was a female sock that came to my knee. It wasn't that my socks were so holey and dirty, it was the fact that, I only owned a few pair and these were the ones I wore the most.

By this time, my dad had walked back over, and when I saw the anger in his face, I burst out crying. He swept me up in his arms and said, "I am not mad at you Pumpkin. "Daddy's not mad at you." He hugged me so tight. "I am just mad at your mama."

When I became a teenager, my mother became a different type of emotional abuser. I now realize she was jealous of me. For all of the things she had done or I had witnessed as a child, none hurt as much as her jealousy of me. I had nothing and she had everything. My father paid child support until I was 18 and I was still going without while she had it all.

My clothing was so limited that I would wear her clothing which were name brand, nice, costly, and in abundance. I practically wore the same things all of the time, rotating the same pairs of jeans and tops as best I could.

When I became pregnant with my son in high school, my mother would tell anyone that would listen that my son, Timothy, belonged to my stepfather. She even told the father of my child's family this lie. I never wanted to believe she would go that low but she did.

The woman who shaped my life and made me who I am, I would have to say is my mother. She is the reason I am who I am today. I embrace and love her because by not wanting to be her, I turned out pretty good.

My children have always been first in my life and everything that I have done and become is so that they would not have memories of me, as I do of my mother. Times were not always easy but my children can never say I had a revolving door of men. My children have only seen me with their father.

My children know that I have always worked hard to take care of them to the best of my ability. Yes, I was tough on them but I know they would not have wanted to endure my upbringing.

My children are far better than I could ever be. I am grateful for every hurt, every pain, and every trying moment in my life. I endured so my three children could be better than me and I am honored to be their mother.

My present glory outside of the greatness of my children is that I have five college degrees and I am currently working on my Doctorate in Educational Leadership. I have written and published my own book. My nonprofit is Striving Spirits, Inc. I have volunteered and worked in my community as a mentor and motivational speaker.

My greatest passion has been working with young African American youth and other minorities. I know what it feels like to be the underdog and to be told that you will never be anything. I know it only takes one person to change your life and make you a better person.

# Chapter Eight

## "The Grand Educational Program
## We Call Life"

*"There is always something to do. There are hungry people to feed, naked people to clothe, sick people to comfort and make well. And while I don't expect you to save the world, I do think it's not asking too much for you to love those with whom you sleep, share the happiness of those whom you call friend, engage those among you who are visionary and remove from your life those who offer you depression, despair and disrespect." – Nikki Giovanni*

### Denise Marcia

As a kid, they loved to frighten and chase me to pinch my short thick thighs playing, "Frankenstein," or they would run from me, screaming, "Cootie-girl!" leaving me crying in the backyard all alone. My sister and two older cousins would many times alienate themselves from me throughout the summers we spent at our relatives' house in Connecticut. I was miserable being away from Mommy, she was my strong tower.

They called me a cry-baby. I thought of myself as "sensitive." Not only were my feelings easily hurt as I was bullied but my sensitivity revealed itself in my body through my childhood allergies: hay fever that had me rhythmically sneezing like a historic locomotive chugging across country, or itchy rashes that would paint my body like red continents on a world map because of my delicate system. I was allergic to the best treats of that time: Bazooka Bubblegum and Jell-O – all flavors! I really think I was allergic to my kid-relatives!

Born and raised in New York, one of two middle children, all of who are girls, our young family of six lived life in the projects of the Bronx. Neither Mom nor Dad had chosen career paths, but made do by taking on very reputable jobs. My earliest memory of my mother's employment was as store detective in retail department stores, Korvette's and Alexander's. She had an eye for wrong doers, which my sister and I knew first hand.

Nothing got past my mother. From our behavior at school, in the playground, or even while she was at work and we were alone, our mother somehow knew when we misbehaved and almost like she was omnipresent, she would recite the incident while she spanked the offending daughter or daughters. Each syllable had its own belt-strike: Did *(whack!)* din't *(whack!)* I *(whack!)* tell *(whack!)* you *(whack!)* not *(whack!)* to *(whack!)*…well, you get the picture! Our little thighs and hands (from shielding our legs) would sting like a million bees as she danced us around the bedroom with daddy's alligator belt, wielding it like Indiana Jones in the Temple of Doom. Today, I'm convinced my mother would have served time, but back then, she put the fear of God and her wrath in us, to do right.

Oh, but our mother loved us fiercely and just as demonstratively, showered us with kisses, hugs, tickles and great games of Hide-and-Seek. She kissed our scraped knees, and our banged heads as she rebuked the violating ground or cabinet with, "Bad floor, or bad door!" that caused her babies' hurt. And we would nod in agreement while wiping our tears, then get a "you're-okay" hug, face washed and Mom's personal attention until something else distracted us to jump off her lap.

Now Daddy was different – a good different! My father graduated from high school and was forced to enlist in the Navy by his mother, a single mom. She knew her son wouldn't make it long hanging out in the streets of New York and she wasn't taking any chances. When daddy finished his tour of duty in WW II, he sought work like every other military person.

Dad loved people and he loved serving them so dad took jobs as a yellow cab driver and as a waiter in New York's jazz clubs. Back then both jobs were very classy – at least our dad made it seem so! He was proud of his work. Dad was a handsome, charming and tasteful man. The bounce he had when he walked was one that flaunted his love of life, his wife and girls. When times were tight dad did whatever was necessary to keep his girls stylishly dressed, and well fed. That was Mommy's edict. So during those times, he even drove a few big rigs!

Daddy loved his girls and thought of us all the time. He always managed to make it home before our 7:30 bedtime, and when we heard his key in the door, we sisters – all four of us, would fall over one another to be the first to hug him. Daddy would let us swing from his strong arms, treating him like an amusement park ride. Then as we stood before him giggle-hopping he would pull out a sweet treat from the small brown paper bag hidden behind his back for each of us: a cup of Breyer's ice cream, or a Clark Bar that would send us excitedly to the floor to enjoy the snack, as Mommy kissed him long – in the mouth…Oooooo! Life was a sweet fairy-tale.

Next thing I knew, we left the Highbridge Projects in the Bronx and re-located to our new home in Connecticut. Mommy said it was to be closer to her family. Then she said my older sister who was about to graduate from high school began jumping the trains into Manhattan and it was time to get us all out of New York. But what was weird was Daddy would come home late now – we were too old for treats, and he would not sleep in his and Mommy's room anymore. Not long after that, dad moved out. It was all very "civil" in our eyes. I don't remember asking why, and I don't know why we kids didn't even think it strange.

Daddy bought a car in Connecticut and taught each of us how to drive. At 16-years-old, I had the privilege of driving the family to dad's mom's house in New York, on the highway. Hands at 10 and 2, and keeping up with the other traffic, we heard a loud "pop" and the power steering went out and forced me to hold the wheel tight. Daddy calmly said, "We had a blow-out, Dedi, hold the wheel, pump the brakes, use your turn signal and ease the car to the side of the road." Mommy started to panic, but Daddy said, "Hush Margaret, she's doing fine, she's doing just fine."

We made it to the side of the road, and I was a hero! Mommy smothered me in kisses, Daddy, "Good job!" My older sister rolled her eyes like it was no big thing. I saved her silly life – me, all by myself! Daddy changed the tire and he drove us the rest of the way into New York, but I was the talk of the dinner table that day. I still smile about it!

My mom's side of the family was very large; Daddy had one sister. Mom was one of six girls and two brothers. I never knew her mother or father, they both passed away before we were born. My mother came from a family of beautiful women, and they gave birth to beautiful children, many of whom were girls too. I gravitated to one of my older female cousins, Beverly who was a very beautiful "girlie-girl." She was a middle child also, and was a master prankster. She knew how to "work her beauty" as she pulled playful stunts on her sister and brother that would have their mother blaming them as Beverly would giggle into her hand. Our country stays were in this house where Beverly and her siblings lived.

She would love to dress up and decorate her face with make-up. Since she was four years older than me, I was mesmerized as I watched her use the short, red Maybelline eyebrow pencil in Blackest-Black to meticulously outline her huge eyes like Cleopatra, and rouge her high cheek bones, as she made a smile-face, then apply cream-colored lipstick to her full, Hershey's-chocolate mouth. I would sit on her bed in awe, and watch Beverly as she stood before her dresser mirror to remove the field of pink sponge rollers from her hair and brush, comb, then brush again her thick, relaxed shoulder-length hair that 'moved' like White people's when she turned her head. Beverly was gorgeous, and I wanted to be just like her, but I was nowhere near as pretty!

Cousin Beverly laughed easily, loved cats, games and silliness, and she had a White boyfriend! Beverly also had an infectious personality that made all people love her, White and Black. Her family lived in the suburbs of Connecticut, purchasing a completely furnished four bedroom, two-bath home that set back from the road with a back yard that yielded 27 apple trees and a huge brick bar-b-que pit. I suppose Black folks would call them rich, and Whites might say, "uppity," since this was the late '50s. I was an adult when I found out, that when my aunt and uncle were interested in purchasing this home they were required to see it at night. Racism was alive in the North too.

While we were considered "lower middle class," my mom's sister and brother-in-law were "upper middle class." Aunt Lou was a teacher and Uncle Prince owned dry cleaners, which enabled them to sock away lots of money. They were almost able to purchase their fabulous house cash. The home was the location for annual, gargantuan family picnics for many years, and is still in the family. My aunt meticulously maintained its Vintage Traditional design the home had when first purchased. Aunt Louise, our family's matriarch, wise, comical and mentally alert as ever recently passed away at the age of 94!

Beverly was a role model for me. As I kept my eyes on her, I adopted her open personality, and friendliness. She had outgrown the silly jokes, thank God, and transformed into a model-esque beauty. She had breasts and a small waist; I was flat as a pancake and would stuff my training bra with toilet paper that made geometric shapes in my tee shirts. Although completely unachievable, I would try anything to be like her!

As kids, Beverly introduced me to the arts. We would often put on showcases for the family using dress-up clothes or Bev's dance outfits. Although dance class wasn't in my family's budget, Beverly taught me what she had learned in hers. And she would put makeup on my face that seemed to make me stand taller and walk softer. I loved playing pretend with Beverly, and she loved teaching me how to be lady-like. She also piqued my interest in acting.

My high school had a drama department; I auditioned for a play, and was cast! Miss Hardy was the acting teacher/director and the first show she cast me in was "Guys and Dolls." It had two tap dance numbers in it and I had no clue how to tap. But there was a cast member, an upper classman named Doris who saw me struggling and frustrated at my own ineptitude in tap. She invited me to her family's apartment with my shiny, new black patent-leather tap shoes, to give me private lessons. Doris patiently and methodically taught me the two tap dances for the show. I remember working so long that my legs would ache as we marked up the kitchen's linoleum floor with our shoes. I, also, remember getting down on hands and knees with steel wool cleaning up those marks before I left!

Miss Hardy and Doris must have seen something in me that I had yet to discover, talent for dance and theatre. But the deeper lessons were these unobtrusive women and my cousin Beverly, impacted my life so greatly, I was on my way to discovering my purpose.

I fell in love with the theatre in high school. Miss Hardy was a no-nonsense kind of teacher and director. A White lady built like a refrigerator, she never complimented anyone about their performance in rehearsal, but she would cuss up a loud storm when someone missed a line and cue or forgot blocking – which is actors' movement on the stage. "NO, DAMMIT! You're supposed to move downstage right!" she would scream from the audience darkness during dress rehearsal. And if the poor student-actor still didn't know his direction, Miss Hardy's visage would emerge from the Blackness to unite with her tirade of obscenities. She and her lit cigarette would appear at the foot of the auditorium stage gesturing ferociously, left arm straight out with cigarette-finger pointing to the area that actor had better hurry up to! No one wanted to have Miss Hardy yell at them, so most of us knew our places. She was gentle and strangely soft as she helped us develop characters during rehearsals. I believe it was the pressure of a soon-coming opening night that turned Miss Hardy into a scary witch.

And as I remember, every play I was in Miss Hardy would "go off the rails," close to opening night, directing us high school students. But, I also, remember our productions receiving accolades from folks like, "This is Broadway material!" time and time again.

I just loved this life! The first Broadway play I ever saw was "Purlie Victorious," with Melba Moore. I don't think I blinked once while sitting in that balcony with the bird's eye view of lights, orchestra, scenery changes, actors and costumes. My life was changed!

As strict and seemingly hostile as Miss Hardy was, she taught us invaluable lessons about the requirement of diligence to achieve excellence – the importance of spending quality time perfecting a craft. When it was graduation time, and I was required to attend college – again Mom's edict, I chose to major in Theatre. No other career field interested me. And so, I was accepted into Howard University's School of Fine Arts, and my life was purposed!

I took my BFA degree from Howard University and was ready to conquer the entertainment industry. My classmate – who was also my best friend, and I took only the clothes we could pack into her small car and we took off from Washington, DC. Since we were both from New York, we decided to brave a brand new world, so Hollywood, California was our destination!

Like the comedy of 'Laverne and Shirley,' and the drama and action of 'Thelma and Louise,' we were a traveling sisterhood. We had a few scandalous adventures on the road that I will not share here. All I can tell you is, had we been older, we would have thought twice about some of the decisions we made during our journey. I remember a saying, 'God looks out for babies and fools.' Today I can only say, Thank you Lord! We had lots of foolish 'fun' before finally spying that very famous Hollywood sign in the hills, some seven days later!

Cousin Beverly had preceded me to Hollywood by a couple years. Yes, I had continued following in her footsteps. And once more she helped me. Introducing me to both her Hollywood commercial and theatrical agents, my professional acting career was launched! Fortunately, I landed several television commercial jobs, and was sent out for some of the big screen movie auditions of that time. I co-starred in a pilot for the ABC network. Although it didn't get "picked up" for a season of airing, I was treated like a Hollywood star during rehearsals and television filming. We shot on Hollywood's renowned Paramount Studios lot. I had my own dressing room and yellow canvas director's chair for 'Denise Marcia.' I foolishly thought myself to have 'made it,' when in fact I was only a momentary working actor.

I had the great fortune to audition with Sidney Poitier, who complimented me on my talent – something I will never forget. What I found out though, Hollywood politics plays a big part in securing acting work. So the part I auditioned for, with Mr. Poitier was given to another ingénue. She was a part of the current-running, Fame TV's.

These were only a couple of my many successes and failures. There were many more, as well as career changes, but for the purpose of this writing I will end there. Having the Lord invade my life brought me to yet another level of gratitude and understanding about love. The way in which that happened is a story in itself! God truly "saved a wretch like me."

As I reflect upon the early and latter parts of my life, the most common thread in it was the realization that nothing gets accomplished apart from relationship. The Senegalese proverb: "When you see a turtle on top of a fence post, you know he had some help," rings loud and clear throughout my life.

In this era of isolationism, our eyes lower to smart-phone glass and our ears embrace small plugs, we have severely reduced our face-to-face interactions. Current generations are satisfied with their few thousand 'virtual' friends and mistakenly call that relationship. I have never had a lot of friends, but the few I have had were mostly women, and each were instrumental in modeling important character traits and also helping me discover who I am.

Growing up in a family of girls, and having oodles of aunties and girl-cousins, I think I have developed a multi-dimensional connectedness to hearts of girls and woman. We possess intuition, fortitude, resilience, and stamina. Many call it, "grit and guts." The problem is, it must be discovered and cultivated. And who better to do that, than other women?

Through a supposed hard or bad time in our lives there is an unfolding of another incredible characteristic of purpose that is ours alone. As we mature and begin to ponder our life, we come to know that each experience – wonderful and terrible, work together to perfect our purpose. The Bible says, "All things work together for good to them that love the Lord and are called according to His purpose." Without being preachy, God created us for His purpose. God is Love and Love only, but, He graciously allows us to make choices about our lives. The decision to embrace or abort our destiny is ours but know this: answering our personal, "Why am I here?" question, discovering and using gifts and skills unique to us is our highest joy.

The journey to purpose has speed bumps, detours, and stop signs. At the intersection of our joys and our successes, we find our purpose. Yes, you will have to adjust and adapt to new ways of being as you become your best self. It's simply part of the process. Purpose is not easy but it is magnificent!

As an adult I now realize my 'sensitivity' and the folly of children's pranks 'worked together' to give me a tenderness toward others who may be emotionally delicate or who may lack confidence. I look for people I can pour into who, like Doris poured into me as we scuffed up her mom's linoleum floor together. I take leadership roles seriously, and like Miss Hardy if you're under my direction you may feel the bite of my pit-bull tenacity for excellence. And also like my cousin Beverly, I model that which I believe, knowing there are "eyes" that are watching me and being influenced by my actions.

My life's purpose is training and coaching people in the rules of social behavior and business protocol. My heart leans more heavily toward our young ladies. Although we are different as snowflakes, we each can learn and practice methods of being respectable, kind, and considerate toward one another. In useful and significant ways, I incorporate my theatrical background to entertain as well as educate, and call it 'edutainment!' One thing I know for sure, you will never be truly happy until you live in your purpose.

# Reflections from the Soul

# Chapter Nine

The Black Woman – Our Cause Speeds Nobly On Its Way,
No Matter What!

*"It's time for you to move, realizing that the thing you are seeking is also seeking you." –*
*Iyanla Vanzant*

## Dr. Cierrah Perrin

Bell Hooks once stated, *"No other group in America has so had their identity socialized out of existence as have Black women. When Black people are talked about the focus tends to be on Black men; and when women are talked about the focus tends to be on White women."*

Being a Black woman in America is like being a part of an exclusive *members only* club. It comes with it its own set of benefits. We are viewed as the backbone of the family, starting from past generations of mothers, who passed down strength to their daughters, then their daughters to their daughters. Black women hold the responsibility of maintaining strength. This unique strength is intrinsically embedded in our DNA. Because of this elaborate strength, Black women tend to endure more than we probably should. Our grandmothers are raising grandchildren, wives are forgiving husbands, mothers are fighting for their children, and the list continues.

The Black woman is a nurturer. We do all we can to keep our family together and we make the best out of what we are given. As a Black woman, we learn fairly early that hard work is mandated, not only within the dynamics of the household, but in society as a whole. We learn early on that we do not have the same advantages as our Caucasian counterparts. With this revelation, a Black woman has a choice, to hustle harder, or to fall below the standard.

Being a part of this *exclusive club* also comes with its own set of societal and internal struggles. Due to our rooted strength, Black women are often overlooked and misunderstood. We cannot be too strong and sure without being categorized as *the angry Black woman;* yet, being too docile is considered weak. Everyday there is a struggle trying to find a healthy medium. Nevertheless, there are internal cultural struggles within this exclusive club that many of us bring as well.

In a day of modern technology, there are so many depictions, perceptions, and stances of the Black woman. With that, comes an internal battle that we all consume. Of course there is still the old adage, light skin vs. dark skin. Presently, the list has expanded to the educated vs. non-educated, reality TV women vs. corporate-employed women, natural hair vs. chemically processed hair, as Black women become more visible, the internal struggles grow. Many of us are personally conflicted of trying not to be put in a stereotypical category, that we inadvertently and subconsciously create a divide between us as a whole. This is a direct result of the stereotypical depictions of Black women.

Societal perceptions and stereotypical assumptions have created a confliction. As a Black woman, society continues to attempt to put us in a category. For example, one is either this type or that type of woman. From commercials to body imaging, modern day society has consciously made it evident that Black women are not the standard. Thus, with all of these different factors that are working against Black women, we have learned to create opportunities and create a lane exclusively reserved for #BlackGirlMagic.

This begs the question, what is Black Girl Magic? The term *Black Girl Magic* was coined as a direct result of what Bell Hooks stated, because "no other group in America has so had their identity socialized out of existence as have Black women…" Black women have learned to create our own opportunities and we are able to do so because we possess a distinctive set of skills and traits that has allowed us to excel. Rosalind Brewer, Ursula Burns, Mellody Hobson – these aren't just names; these are giants in Corporate America. Who might I add, also happen to be Black women.

The principle lesson that comes with being a Black woman is learning that we can make a difference right where we are, with what we have. Learning to get out of our own way (mentally). We are not encouraged to go against what is seemingly the societal "norm." Every family is different; some are raised with the idea of following their dreams and creating their own path, others are not. Black women are inspired to march to the beat of our own drum. Most importantly, we have to discipline ourselves to listen to that inner voice of discernment that tells us what we're supposed to be doing.

That lays the foundation that allows us to find our distinctive rhythm in a world that tends to overlook us. As a result, we begin to thrive in various phases of our lives. Our culture has afforded us the idealistic truth that every individual has a distinct purpose in this life. As little girls, we had ideas, we planned, studied, and dreamed of all the ways we can effectively obtain that purpose.

However, the idealistic transforms to realistic and then life presents challenges and impediments that distort our belief that our individual purpose is not so attainable. As we overcome our unbelief, we look to others who have successfully accomplished their purpose we have yet to achieve ourselves.

However, where are our books of *sheros?* Why is it, that we do not get to see them on television or portrayed in the media as successful women? Consequently, before the image of Michelle Obama was made visible, we were not afforded the privilege of having a laundry list of individuals that inspired us to re-claim our focus, endure through the pessimism and continue to work harder, and more diligently, to achieve our purpose.

Often times, we look to perfect something or someone however, this is a disillusioned perception. Searching for perfection will continuously leave one disappointed. Perfection is non-existent, but as long as we are exploring the option to continuously progress our view, is more in a realistic state. Even those at their best are not perfect, and trusting on the fact that one day, we will someday, reach a point of perfection is a misguided fact. With so much against us, so many Black women get misguided by the illusion of perfection and can easily derail their journey.

Many of us are learning to accept that we cannot be perfect. Through trial and error, we welcome mistakes as stepping-stones to experience. We are grasping the concept that we do not have to be so hard on ourselves when we fall short of what we say we are all about. Discipline is the key to growth; but learning oneself is a better teacher than anything. Through trial and error, we learn to become the best woman we can be.

Experience is the best teacher, though the tuition is high, we progress in the midst of it all. The wall does not come before laying the bricks. We lay the bricks one by one to create the wall. Greatness is a building process. Having control of our destiny and living a positive life that promotes progression is the biggest gift that we not only give ourselves, but others around us as well.

The accomplishments of Black women often affect those around us. Thus, we release a domino effect of raising the bar, improving the standards. Many of us do not realize that there is always someone paying attention to us, holding admiration. People like this do not expect for us to be perfect, but just to be ourselves, which seemingly becomes inspiration for them. As a direct result, our vision becomes a bit clearer a little more concise.

The dynamics of a vision hold true beauty. As we go through our journey in life we tend to get more direction that puts us on the right track to our vision. However, often times many Black women put ourselves second while making sure our husbands, children, siblings, have their opportunities first. This goes back to the point of Black women being the backbone of the Black family. Then one day, after we are tired and through taking care of everyone else, it clicks. From that point forward, we put forth a valiant effort to make that vision become a reality.

During that journey to successfully ensure that our dreams come to fruition, we encounter some bright days attached with some dark nights. Occasionally, the dark nights are more numerous than the counter opposite. Our faith is tested and sometimes we wonder if our dream is even worth fighting for anymore. We start to wonder if we're good enough and have what it takes. However, there's still a small voice – a strong potency within us – that does not allow the dream to die.

At this point, we start to change the way we think. We continuously focus on self, and the things that make us happy. We learn to push forward and dive deeper into our everyday hustle. Soon, our efforts pay off in dividends. After all of the ups and downs and thinking at times that we would never remotely reach the desires of our heart, we find ourselves realizing that our vision is starting to become a reality. This is creating #BlackGirlMagic.

When we finally reach a point where we have our morals, priorities, goals, and aspirations in sync; we try our hardest not to drift back to old habits or people that we had to let go. Retrograde is a state of movement only meant for planets. As Black women, when we tap into something that we once let go, it compares to reopening a healed womb. Thus, it is imperative that we are consistent with who we are and where we stand. In order to continuously prosper, we have to stand firmly on what we believe and who we are as women. Constantly going back and forth with things and people who serve us no good and is a pure waste of time. However, we often toy with the idea that we can save those around us.

With that being said, we are left with two options in life; to be a stand up woman and stand firmly on those values or have a seat. Some of us had to learn the hard way that no one will respect a person who cannot make up their mind regarding who they are. If you do not know who you are, how do you expect other people to figure it out? It takes a lifetime to fully learn oneself; however, we must establish a starting point on where we can start directing our lives in a way that is beneficial to us. Life is such a great tool to keep learning more and more about who we are; we dictate to the people whom we deal with, and most importantly, our purpose.

Black women often struggle with the old saying "not forgetting where we come from." Believing in oneself is the most important thing. At times we allow idealistic perceptions, people, and society to make us hesitate who we are. We do not want to separate ourselves from our culture, but we also do not want to fall victim to all the stereotypical facades. We have to learn not to turn down our ambition because people are not happy with the volume.

Personal Reflection: I have been blessed to have many aunts in my life. Thus, I have viewed the personality traits and characteristics of many different women. I have seen it all – the passive, the aggressive, the volatile, and the submissive. At a young age, I started to realize what I wanted to stand for, what my signature would signify. I would state a blatant lie if I state that I have it all figured out. I know I have to be committed to my goals, but flexible in my approach. Actually, I learn something new about myself every day. Yet, I know my limitations, I know what I believe in, I know where my morale stands, and I believe that I can accomplish anything in which I am committed.

Not too long ago, my dad told me that I was not born with a silver spoon in my mouth. My response to him was that I know that I was not, nonetheless, my journey in life is totally contingent upon my actions. I know where I stand with my goals and aspirations; I know who I am as a woman and where I want to be. At that moment, I stood for what I believed in–I did not choose to take a seat.

It is important that we do not ignore words of wisdom because we feel as if they do not apply to us this season; just wait, those very words may be exactly what you need to hear next season. Wisdom is always in season. It is pertinent that we keep an open mind about personal growth. We can never grow too much, thus, if we are doing well and people are complimenting us more than usual, give thanks, but know that success is not contingent upon what people think of you. More so, if things take a turn for the worse and those compliments come far and in between and those same fans become critics, as women, we have to discover not how to define ourselves by either.

One thing that I learned that it is unhealthy to live my life based on the presence of critics or fanatics. I have to live according to what I think is best for me. If we become too reliable on being highly praised, it can easily lead us into a state of arrogance and self-centeredness that we once did not possess. On the other hand, if we become reliable on critics from others, it can easily lead to a state of insecurity; and being an insecure woman is something that can always be avoided just by remaining self-assured and open to wisdom. Life has taught me that it is a weakness to be so consumed in what others think of me that I compromise my true self and who I really am. Characters are only essential in movies and books, I have to be who I am and stand by it. I contemplated, if I had to meet myself, would I like who I met? Remaining true to oneself through the highest and lowest points are ways to avoid this weakness. If we learn to remain sure about who we are, we will never need confirmation from others.

I come from a two-parent household of high-school educated parents. My father worked six days a week and my mom was a domestic homemaker. I know that they did the best they did with what they had. We were not impoverished; neither were we wealthy. At a young age I was idealistic and curious. I had dreams about who I would become and what I would accomplish. However, with all these dreams in me, no one ever told me how to start. Make good grades was what I was told. My dad made it clear that was my way out. As a result, I excelled in the public school system. I was able to earn a partial scholarship to Alabama State University.

There it was, at 17, I left home for college and that is when my journey began. I was an average student in college. No one told me that average grades would make it very hard for me to get into law school. No one in my family had ever attended law school. I was at the top of my class in high school, however, my young arrogant mindset made me believe I could keep the same habits and still thrive. It was not until my junior year that I realized I had to work twice as hard to get into law school. I enrolled in the Kaplan course, which was not offered in Montgomery, AL at the time. Every Tuesday and Thursday after class, I would drive to Birmingham for my LSAT course. I was determined to make my dream become a reality.

Then came law school in Chicago. I was accepted to The John Marshall Law School Chicago, on a contingency. After I completed the summer course, I was enrolled into the Intellectual Property Law program, which was one of the best in the country. No one warned me that my parents would be going through a bitter divorce and it would weigh heavily on my grades. I, sometimes, wonder myself how I made it out. Most of my years in

Chicago I was depressed and withdrawn from my family and friends. It was easier for me to cope being alone. I was angry and I was hurt. I didn't know what to do, so I made a decision to move, again.

After graduation, I was accepted into the Organizational Leadership Program for the Ed.D. at Argosy University, Chicago. That summer, I moved to Atlanta. I needed a new start. I decided to no longer dwell on the past and my parents' decision. I decided that this life was mine to live and I needed to tap into my purpose.

Being a little girl from East Nashville, I never really understood the power that I possessed. Anything that I have envisioned for myself, a higher authority has blessed me with the tools and the skills to ensure that I can accomplish. The road was not easy. There were several setbacks and times that I just wanted to give up and scream. In addition, sometimes it is hard for family and friends to understand how you can come from the same place as them and end up so differently. My answer is simple, choices.

We are all extended the same courtesy of making our life choices. Though I am guilty of not always making the right choice, I have learned from the ones that did not work out in my favor. Life has not been easy. There hasn't been a roadmap with caution signs. By the grace of God, I have been blessed with the spirit of discernment. I try not to rush opportunities and I now know that I cannot skip the struggle.

At the age of 30, I was awarded my doctoral degree. I'm employed at a top information technology firm, I own a small business, Perrin Professional Group, and I'm an associate professor at two universities. Sometimes I reminisce of where I was. I thank God from saving me from what I thought I wanted. I now know that every mistake, lesson, roadblock, and perceived hindrance were all building blocks to who I am.

Being a Black woman in information technology isn't easy. Like the other aspects of life, it's a constant struggle with proving myself. However, it's good for me. I work hard, and I am constantly challenged. I know that all of my efforts will pay off and somehow make a difference. Corporate, for me is good for the ego, but when I am in front of my MBA students in the classroom, now that's good for the soul.

I'm honored that God made me a Black woman. I'm multi-faced and I have so many inner strengths that I get to tap into on a daily basis. I have met life's challenges and know that there will be so much more ahead. However, the revelation was realizing that it's not about me. It's about all of those other little girls across the world. Everything positive that comes from a Black woman will affect them. I'm honored to know that I contribute to the greater good. I love possessing my #BlackGirlMagic.

# Chapter Ten

## Stay Alert, Stay Alive For The
## Element Of Surprise

*"Courage is the most important of all the virtues, because without courage you can't practice any other virtue consistently. You can practice any virtue erratically, but nothing consistently without courage."* – Maya Angelou

### Brittany Shook

There I was, listening to the voice on the other end of the phone telling me; "sorry Ms. Shook but it doesn't look good, the biopsy shows that you have cancer." I know we all have a story but at twenty-seven I never imagined this to be a part of mine. Up until that phone call, I felt that my life was pretty normal. I felt that I hadn't had anymore or any less hardships or disappointments than the next person.

I was born and raised to a humble middle-class family in East Nashville. My parents bought their home in East Nashville back in the early 80's; I have personally witnessed the transformation of the area. My mom has worked in Pathology/Histology all of my life and my dad was in the Air Force for over thirty years. My mom had a few miscarriages before me so my parents did not have me until they were in their 30s. My mom was placed on bed rest at three months and at birth her doctors deemed me the "miracle baby". I was able to attend preschool and kindergarten at local Historically Black Colleges and Universities so my foundation started with me knowing that I had Black Girl Magic. I went to Meharry Preschool and Tennessee

State University Early Learning Center. Seeing young Black men and women go to class everyday and even come into my classrooms was the norm to me. I remember learning about Sojourner Truth at Tennessee State Early Learning Center and keeping a picture of her on the refrigerator. Elementary through Middle School I attended predominantly Black schools such as St. Vincent De Paul and Wharton Arts Magnet Middle School. St. Vincent wasn't your typical Catholic school but I learned a lot going there; I was able to see Black Nuns, Sisters, and a Priest. My paternal grandmother, aunt and some paternal great aunts attended there as well so I was next in line.

Although I had gone to a Catholic school my family was Baptist and Primitive Baptist; talk about two completely different extremes. Going to Mass on Wednesdays and Church on Sundays along with being an inquisitive child anyway made me question God at an early age – I always had to know why or how.

Growing up my parents always encouraged me to think for myself and allowed me to share my views and opinions. I remember drawing a family portrait and not getting in trouble for gluing it to the living room wall. People would come over and think 'what in the world', but my parents didn't take it down. My parents had a relaxed parenting style; good behavior was rewarded/acknowledged and bad behavior wasn't tolerated. I didn't fear my parents but respected them so I tried to be the best representation of my household that I could be. My household was filled with love. Friday nights my mom would watch my dad beat me in games of Checkers and Saturdays would be dedicated to whatever activity I was in. I would boohoo and get so mad that my dad would beat me—like, aren't parents supposed to let their kids win? Those Friday night games taught me life lessons and helped build my character. My dad taught me that life is unpredictable and that nothing would be given to me without hard work. His firmness gave me my thick skin. My mom was and is our family's cheerleader, nurturer, referee, and voice of reason. Her love, patience and calmness made whatever worry or problem go away. I'm a lot like my dad and can be hot headed at times but my mom taught me that everything doesn't need a response. Her existence and the way she loves is why I believe there's a God. Some would say my mom babied me but the gentleness of my mom and the firmness of my dad made a great combination – it provided me an array of ways to deal with the world and all of its challenges.

High school was the first time I used the "Black card". I wanted to go to a public school, however my zoned high school was not up to par. My parents got me a 'Majority to Minority" special transfer to a high school in another district. I had a lot of first time experiences in high school. I was the new girl so I experienced shade from some of the other girls; I experienced the most shade from other Black girls. I was asked, why do I talk the way I do? I remember one girl saying, "The only reason I had nice things was because my parents' were old."

I wasn't like the White girls and I wasn't like other Black girls, I was just me. I was intrigued by the different nationalities and ethnicities I encountered at school; it was beyond White and Black. This was the first time I had friends that were not just Black – I had Mexican friends, Kurdish friends, Somali friends, Indian friends, West Indian friends and the list goes on. I took my first international trip in high school. My Honors English teacher would take a trip abroad every summer and the year I went, we toured Italy for about two weeks. I was the only person from my class that went as well as the only Black person. My parents told me they would match whatever I saved for spending money. That year I got my first job at Popeye's Chicken and Biscuits. (I haven't eaten a piece of Popeye's Chicken since.) High School was where I first felt wanderlust.

I received academic and minority scholarships to a few different colleges but I chose to go to the University of Tennessee Chattanooga; this would be the second time I used the "Black card." At that time, UTC wanted to diversify their campus more so they gave all type of diversity and minority money out. College was cool. I was away from home but not too far; I was doing well in my classes and life was great. However, one of the shifts in my life came during my sophomore year of college. My parents were starting their divorce, I started an unhealthy relationship with a guy, my grades dropped because I stopped going to class and I lost my scholarships. I thought the divorce of my parents had no affect on me but that was a lie. I said that I would rather see them apart as friends than together as enemies. I really felt that way but the truth of the matter was/is divorces affect children regardless of if they are 9 years old or 19.

My college ex was a stand out basketball player and had many female fans. I put up with things that I knew I shouldn't have put up with. Instead of facing my parents' divorce head on, I ran from it – I avoided it by staying in a relationship that was unhealthy. I dealt with drama from his child's mother who lived in another state as well as drama from an ex of his that was a local. The drama was through the roof. I would receive random phone calls, attacks on social media from the young lady, her friends and family; I was even followed home a few times.

I was so depressed during that time but didn't know it. I lost a lot of weight and was overall lost. He and I would argue all of the time but he would make it up to me by buying me gifts. I started to associate him caring for me/loving me with the gifts he got me. Our relationship was pretty much fights and gifts. It would be he and I arguing or me arguing with the 'baby mama' or ex girlfriend. I tried to justify it by saying he's a college athlete so this stuff must come with the territory. I had other people in my ear saying to stay in the relationship because what if he goes pro or overseas.

The summer of my sophomore year was when everything hit the fan; I went against my better judgment and stayed in Chattanooga with my ex instead of going back home. I was trying to get closer to God but it seemed the closer I tried to get, more bad stuff would happen. Summer school didn't work out. I started receiving threats. My ex wasn't there for me like I felt he should have been. I didn't want to go home – the depression, loneliness and sadness was times 10. The drama eventually became physical with the young lady and her friends and I ended up getting an aggravated assault charge. My whole world was upside down. I wasn't raised this way; I had never even seen anyone go through what I was going through so why did I think it was acceptable.

Unfortunately, that event was my wake up call. I told myself this can't be life. I wasn't destined to stay in an unhealthy relationship, I wasn't created to live in a life of depression and I wasn't made to pointlessly fight with people who had nothing to lose. I ended the relationship, packed my bags and went home to my mama. It was such a relief to be back home in a truly loving environment.

Things were getting better but I still had an aggravated assault charge. For some reason every time I was threatened or attacked on social media, I printed it off and I had police reports of when I was followed home; all of this is what saved me along with being a college student with no previous record. I had to go back and forth to court for a year and I saw first hand how the judicial system worked/didn't work for Black people. No matter how nice of a resume I had, I couldn't get a job because I was charged with a felony. I enrolled in Nashville State to try to undo the damage I had done to my GPA. I will admit that at first I was embarrassed. How could someone who had scholarships to multiple four-year universities be back at what I considered square one? I quickly got off my high horse and graduated with an Associates degree in Business Information Systems. Fortunately, my parents were able to hire a good lawyer. My charges were dropped to simple assault and I received a pre-trial diversion with six months of unsupervised probation.

My life was finally back on track. After graduating with an Associates degree, I enrolled at Middle Tennessee State University. At times, I would get upset with myself because I saw my friends graduating who I started out with in 2006. I would get angry with myself for allowing certain things to transpire in my life. In 2012, I finally graduated with my Bachelors. I walked in May but as life would have it, I was emailed in June saying one of my prerequisite classes from 2006 didn't count. I needed one class to complete my degree. I enrolled in an online class and received my degree in December of 2012.

During that time, I started my first full time 'big girl' job. I started working for a global insurance company in their IT department. I didn't think I would get the job because the other candidate had her masters and I was still completing my Bachelors. The other candidate was hired almost immediately, but two weeks later I received a call back stating they wanted to hire me as well. In addition to that, my boss told me that as long as my work was completed on time, I could do my course work to complete my degree while on the clock. I started out being really nervous about corporate world politics – like how do I laugh at jokes that aren't funny? How do I handle awkward situations? How do I say, *just because I'm Black I am not the spokesperson for all things that are considered to be Black?* How do I hide my large behind without looking sloppy and can I take my weave out and wear my hair in its natural state? I loved my job at first. The VP and assistant VP of my department were both women; they lived in DC and would come in monthly. The assistant VP was Puerto Rican. She took another young Black woman and myself under her wing, which I am forever grateful. Seeing and being able to interact with women in high positions gave me something to strive for.

However, after about a year I was over it. I felt that I was becoming complacent; I felt that my life was becoming a revolving door of work and happy hour. I needed something new, I needed to be out of my comfort zone, and I needed the fire inside of me to become lit again. A friend of mine who lived in China asked me to come visit. Plans fell through with that trip but I still wanted to go. I had been looking and applying for jobs in every region of the US but would always get, "I'm sorry but we are looking for someone with more experience." Since I still wanted to go to China, I said, hey instead of me paying to go to China, why don't I find a way to get paid to go to China.

I researched and researched until I stumbled upon a young lady's Instagram who was an American teacher in China. Ironically, she and my cousin were friends. I found a company that offered a 5-month cultural exchange program. I would teach as well as participate in cultural events. Because life is unpredictable, I encountered problems with obtaining the correct visa. I thought, Lord is this a sign that I shouldn't go. I had already quit my job so I told myself, *find a way to make it work.* I didn't know Mandarin or anyone in China but in January of 2014, I took a giant leap of faith and moved to Chengdu, China. It was one of the best decisions I've ever made.

Five months turned into a year and a half. I could write a book on my experience in China alone. I met and became friends with many wonderful people. You would think I would have become close friends with more Chinese people but I didn't; I was in awe of the Blackness around me. I now have Black friends from Italy, London, Benin, Namibia, Ghana, South

Africa, Brazil and Tanzania. I kind of envied my friends from Africa. They spoke multiple languages. They had a culture, and even though they were from different countries they had this bond and you could feel it. I gained a greater independence and strength. I had to fight with a previous employer for money owed to me, I had to find an apartment on my own, I had to communicate and get around in a place that spoke little English, and I started to travel to other Southeast Asian countries by myself.

In April of 2015, I decided not to renew my contract in China. I took a month vacation and decided to come back to America mid May. My plans were to go get a physical to check out a knot I felt in my breast and to start a job in Mexico late June. I got checked out. The doctors did an ultrasound of my breast and I was told everything was fine. I was told that the knot I was feeling was a fibro adenoma. The nurse was more concerned about the possibility of me having Ebola, although I didn't have any symptoms of Ebola.

My family and friends asked me to reconsider Mexico, which I did. The money didn't add up so I declined the offer. I applied for jobs here and there. I had an interview in New York for an airline in Dubai starting immediately but nothing was working out.

I got a second opinion about my breast; I received the same answer. It was the end of July now and I started to worry about what I was going to do as far as employment. August came; my mom was still pressed about the knot in my breast. She told my sister who just so happens to work for an oncology office what was going on. My sister told the doctor that she worked for about me and they had me come into the office. I was a little irritated because this was now my third doctor's visit. My insurance stopped once I left China. Obamacare denied me and I was paying for everything out-of-pocket. I didn't have any potential job leads.

I went to my sister's job and just handed them the same results the other two doctors looked at. The nurse practitioner looked at them and told me they wanted to refer me to a surgeon just to be on the safe side. I pushed back the date of my first appointment and was stopped dead in my tracks as I was going to push it back again. One day as I was getting ready I dropped my deodorant stick and instead of getting a new stick, I just rubbed on a piece of the deodorant with my fingers. As I got to my left side, I felt another knot but this time it was under my arm and it could only be felt when my arm was in a certain position. I knew a knot under my arm could only be two things, so I had a biopsy performed.

As I said before, life is unpredictable. On August 25, 2015, I listened to the voice on the other end of the phone tell me "sorry Ms. Shook but it doesn't look good, the biopsy shows that you have cancer." I felt every emotion at that moment. I was in shock – I laughed, I cried, I got mad that they told me over the phone. I was mad that two previous doctors, months before, told me I was fine and to come back in six months.

I went back to the surgeon's office. He informed me that from the growth rate of the tumors it appeared that I had cancer for seven and a half years and didn't know it. The doctor my sister worked for said she would be my oncologist and that I would never see a bill from her office. I remember for the most part I was good in spirits, I had only been told that I had cancer and thought that everything would be over by January 2016; talk about wishful thinking.

My oncologist informed me that not only did I have Invasive Ductal Carcinoma, but also it was Stage III with lymph node involvement. How could I at twenty-seven, have Stage III Breast Cancer? At that moment I told myself I was only going to give cancer six months of my life, realistically I knew it would be longer. One of the few times I cried in front of anyone was when the doctor told me I would lose my hair after my first chemotherapy treatment. To save myself the agony of seeing my hair fall out in big chunks, I decided to cut my hair off. My mom and I cut our hair into baby Afros. I looked at my cancer journey as a total body detox. I was getting rid of everything negative in my life. I looked at cancer as my opportunity to start fresh. I had to learn to love myself again – and to embrace my bald head.

I realized that I was scared to be me. In the past you would have never caught me without some type of hair weave. I had been whitewashed by society. I had natural hair under my weave, but felt unattractive wearing it. I had a bilateral mastectomy with lymph node dissection. I once again lost something that society says makes me a woman. I now embrace my scars and keep it rolling. Cancer taught me to fight for my life, like my life depended on it. I've made decisions regarding my treatment that my doctors didn't agree with like receiving a form of radiation called Proton Therapy. I've even had to fight with my insurance company to get them to pay for things. I research, I go to lectures about Breast Cancer, I volunteer at different cancer nonprofits so that I can be informed, because the truth of the matter is the same information and resources aren't given to us.

Not only has my mom been my caregiver and co-survivor but she has also been my role model through out my journey. She's like superwoman to me. She can do any job a man can do, bake the heck out of some chess squares as well explain the microscopic anatomy of the lung of a mouse. She's had a lot of hardships in life but still manages to love others selflessly. She's my biggest supporter, my shoulder to cry on, and my best friend. If no one else loves me in this world, I know she does.

My Aunt Thea has been one of my role models as well, she reminds me of a younger version of my mom. My Godmother Cordelia is another one of my role models; she's straight to the point and assertive. She doesn't know this but my friend Adero is also my role model. She's from Chicago but we met in China, I have yet to meet anyone as determined as she is. She's had a few hardships in life but she has not let any of them stop her. She was born without a full right arm but plays the violin beautifully. While I was contemplating moving back to America because of my hair, she chopped her's off, dyed it lilac and owned it – and she can talk to you about Tolstoy or Trap Music.

My role models have supported me, influenced me and helped me throughout my journey. When I need uplifting, they uplift me, which is essential for my growth. It's essential for other Black women I encounter to know – *hey, sister you have a friend in me.* I can't be a woman of worth or the woman of my dreams if I can't uplift my own sister. We as Black women have to start showing love to one another. We must realize that life is about transitioning and advancement and if one succeeds we all succeed. We have to let go of past hurt and aim higher than the negative stereotypes that are placed upon us. We are more than the hair pulling and name-calling women on Basketball Wives or Love and Hip Hop. We are the most neglected, unprotected and disrespected people in America, so why not be each others moral support.

I feel that my journey calls for me to uplift Black women affected by Breast Cancer. Black women have the highest mortality rate. We are less likely to receive reconstruction surgery; we are the least insured but the most likely to fall victim to disparities in health care. As a survivor, it is my job to educate and inform other young Black women. I was given and survived Breast Cancer for a reason. I will not let my journey go in vain.

# Chapter Eleven

Who Am I, Who Are You?

*"We are all gifted. That is our inheritance."*
– *Ethel Waters*

## Dr. Cheryl Green

Black----Woman----Woman who is Black----Black who is woman Black woman.........I would definitely have to say that there is no one emotion that captures all of the feelings experienced by me while living in this Black body called "wo-man." While living as a Black woman in America for over fifty years, I have felt a myriad of emotions. Sometimes I have had distinct feelings about being a woman and sometimes I have had unique feelings about being Black. But in reality, I have always been both Black and Female. I have not always been a woman. I have been a "Little Sister, Girl, Young Lady, and then a Woman." Womanhood is something that you grow into being. You evolve as a Black woman. It's developmental, spiritual, magical, powerful and inevitable.

I cannot list every feeling that I have had as a Black woman but some of the positive human emotions that I have felt are love, joy, pride, serenity, pleasure, compassion, passion, gratitude, satisfaction, excitement, kindness, amazement, surprise, peace, and yes I have even felt blessed over and over and over again.

But, when I think about the horrific things done to My People, My Culture and My Ancestors during the transatlantic slave period and since then, there is a range of negative feelings that come to mind: anger, sadness, fear, rage, rebellion, hate, guilt, shame, disgust, despair, confusion, jealousy, distrust, tension, inferiority, paralysis, vulnerability, emptiness, terrified, agonized, mournful, disillusioned, violated and just downright oppressed.

How does anyone manage to survive, let alone thrive feeling this broad range of emotions? I started my quest for survival in my mother's womb. You see I was born as an identical twin. Imagine the joy and elation my parents and I felt when I came out of my mother's womb first! My twin sister had breathing complications as a result of a difficult delivery. She later died after a few weeks. She never came home. Her death was never really talked about in much detail. I am certain that this was too painful a topic for my mother and father. I feel somewhat special and privileged to have survived the trauma of birth. Surprisingly, I have never felt guilt about being the one that did survive.

Later in life, during my twenties, I participated in group therapy while in college. I discovered that since I lost my sister at birth, I have spent a great majority of my life looking for and expecting sisterhood from my female friends, relatives and colleagues. I think this quest for sisterhood has shaped my political, professional and spiritual agenda.

## "Little Sister"

"Little Sister" is who I was to my big sister Renee, and the name is also a throwback to a Southern term of endearment for Black girls. After coming into this world as a surviving twin, I then joined the family of my mother, father and older sister. My parents divorced around the time that I was five or six years old. I think that this was the time that I grew even more attached to my sister. My sister is one year and three months older than me. When we were very young, strangely enough, people thought we were twins. It was during this time that my big sister "Nay Nay" was my rock, teacher, protector, role model, partner in crime, etc.

I remember when I started kindergarten; my mother was working three jobs to take care of us. I learned then that hard work is vital to your survival. She hired a full time caretaker to look after us. We called her "Miss

Mousie". I also learned that as a Black woman, when your man fails you and the family, you have to pick up the pieces, take control of the situation and get the job done…whatever the job is at hand. I am sure that for my mother, this left her feeling relieved, saddened, bitter and determined. At least, these are my conclusions. As I write this short auto-ethnography, I am gaining even more insight into my own life. I believe these are all the same feelings that I experience when one of my love relationships ends. This lesson would be one that I followed numerous times throughout my lifetime. It has served as a source of resilience and survival for me and as a psychological barrier for the men in my life. In other more simple words, it has kept me going all these years and it has held me back in many ways for as many years.

In spite of some obvious disappointments, I also have very fond memories of being in school during my pre-adolescent years. One of my earliest and most special memories is having my own library card at the age of six years old and crossing the street with my sister to exchange books. I felt a sense of pride and empowerment to flash my library card, select my own books and check them out. I don't think they allow children that same age to check out their own books without some type of supervision today, but I remember it well. I also had great fears and quasi-nightmares over books that were lost and the charges due for overdue books. It must have been great to be so young and have that as your only major fear in life at that time. I am also sure this was the beginning of me believing and thinking that my intelligence was a concrete factor of my identity.

A similar story involves my being a member of the "Junior Great Books Society." I received a set of bound books that were purple and they contained some of the great literary works by European authors. At this very young and tender age, I was not yet aware of the books authored by Africans or African Americans and I certainly was not taught about Black authors in the Chicago Public School System. I was reading the Old Man and the Sea, Aesop's Fables and the Brothers Grimm, etc. as a young child. I recently learned that in Chicago during 1968, that was the first year that the Junior Great Books Society opened up the readership to include programming for third and fourth graders. I had such pride of ownership for those books.

Strangely enough, I now lecture college students about how our ancestors were denied the right to an education and about how reading was punishable by death during slavery. Because of those historical atrocities, I feel especially entitled to my educational development and have committed my life to helping others become educated formally and informally.

## "Girl"

During my pre-adolescence and teen years, I grew up on the South Side of Chicago. There were many social/cultural/political movements evolving in our community at that time. There were street gangs such as the El Rukns, Gangster Disciples, and Black P. Stone Rangers, Black Nationalist movements and Civil Rights movements all emerging during that time period. Luckily, I grew up thinking and feeling that "Black is Beautiful". I listened to lyrics like "Say It Loud, I'm Black and I'm Proud" by James Brown. During my developmental years, Chicago was a major cultural mecca for Black art, Black literature and Black politics, in spite of the influences of the Jim Crow South, segregation, and institutionalized racism. There were activities, icons and opportunities that helped me to have a solid foundation for developing as a "Black" girl.

There are all kinds of development one has to go through to evolve into being a girl and then a woman. It is a well-established biological fact that one of the key areas of development involves the brain and the limbic system. This is the major area of the brain that controls emotions. For a young heterosexual girl, early emotional and sexual feelings about the men in her life tend to begin with her first significant male figure, her father.

My biological parents divorced when I was about 5 years old. When my father divorced my mother, I think it must have felt like he divorced me too. I have always known that my father loves me. He has never stopped calling, visiting and taking us on family outings, with his second wife and children.

However, there were sooooooo many times that he called, said he would be by to pick us up and never showed. My sister and I lived for those outings. We dressed up, sat on the front porch and braced when every car came down the street. After a few hours of waiting, we would go back in the house, dejected and saddened. I now know that these early experiences set the stage for my general fear of abandonment by men.

Luckily, as I have studied psychology and participated in psychotherapy, I gained this insight as a young woman and later confronted my father about his shortcomings. It was a signature event in our relationship that allowed me to heal emotionally in that special place and grow even closer to him. It was then that I first learned that our parents are not perfect people. They have flaws and more importantly, we all do.

In spite of this early emotional separation trauma that occurred within my immediate family, I had what I consider to be a great childhood. Yes. It had pain, sorrow, tears, joys, victories, achievements and celebrations. I was never left alone as a child, except when playing outside with other children. We had constant care from either my mother, or from a hired caretaker. It was during this time that my big sister "Nay Nay" was my rock, teacher, protector, role model, partner in crime, etc.

My extended family was very close and we often spent weekends at one of my three aunt's homes in Chicago. I love all of my aunts dearly and their children. I had a total of six aunts. Their names are Josie B, Willa Mae, Val, Anne, Doris, and Marva. Five of my aunts lived in Chicago. Four were from the marriage of my maternal grandparents and two more were from my grandfather's earlier romantic unions. Three of them are now deceased. I know that I learned something about being a woman from each one of the four. My aunt Doris was considered to be the best dresser and most stylish one. She owned her own hair salon, home and real estate property. From her I learned that you need to invest in the care and style of your appearance.

My aunt Anne, never worked a traditional job outside the home. She was at one time during my childhood, the best cook in the family. She could cook any southern dish from scratch and have your mouth watering. From her I learned that a woman should know how to cook and do it well. She was also the one who would "kill a brick" about her family.

My aunt Marva is the one who taught me to love everybody. She was the youngest of my mother's siblings. When my sister and I went south for school or vacations, she took care of us as if we were her own children, until she got married and had her own. She tells everybody, we were her "first" babies and because of this, we hold a special place in her heart. I think her own children would beg to differ but I like to believe this is true, especially now that my own mother passed away a few years ago. From my collective experiences with my aunts, I learned that women should love each other. This type of love is not sexual; it's familial, spiritual and psychological. It is normal to love people who look like you; live near you and to whom you share a common ancestry. If this does not happen, it can be assumed that this "un-love" was learned and needs to be unlearned in order to be corrected.

At one point during my developmental years my mother and my aunt Val, were very close and both had a profound effect on my social, political and psychological development. Aunt Val was and still is a pioneer in the Black Arts Movement of the 1960s, 70s, 80s and 90s. She and several others, including Francis Ward, her husband and my mother, founded the "Kuumba Theatre" in Chicago, Illinois in 1968. It was the first Black owned community theatre in the city of Chicago. I include this historical and cultural event because it had a major impact on my own development and consciousness.

Starting at the age of around five years old, I saw the most prominent Black people in America in my aunt's living room. People like Nikki Giovanni, Sonja Sanchez, Mari Evans, Lerone Bennett, Haki Madhubutti (aka Don L. Lee), Amiri Baraka (aka LeRoi Jones), and of course, the Poet Laureate of Illinois and internationally known writer, Mrs. Gwendolyn Brooks. Aunt Val was and still is a writer, producer, director and Emmy Award winning actress. These Black literary giants were her best friends, comrades in the struggle for civil rights and emerging luminaries in their own right. In my aunt's house, I saw statues of Black busts, original oils and charcoal prints, and hundreds of books by Black authors about Black life. I did not receive this education on Black life from my primary education in the public schools. I got it straight from the source(s). I ate with, hung around, watched, listened to and tried to emulate some of the greatest Black thinkers and writers of the 20th century.

I had the larger social society sending one set of negative and destructive messages through the television and print media, and my extended family sending very different messages. My relatives told me I was "beautiful, smart and strong." Maybe I was told this because at the age of fourteen, I graduated as the number one student (valedictorian) of my eighth grade class. I think I knew then, that I was smart and that this was important. I have to state at this time, that I don't believe that I and others are born smart. My studies in psychology have indicated that some people are born with a sort of gift of intellectual aptitude but most of us had to earn good grades the old fashioned way, we had to put the work, hours and sweat in.

When it came to my looks, boys often told me I was" fine". Female friends always complimented me on my looks and my style of clothing. What does this have to do with a Black woman's feelings? Part of your self-concept is related to your self-image. Self-concept also includes beliefs, opinions, attitudes and self-perceptions. I believe that any discussion that involves a focus on the feelings of being a Black woman, must include the powerful impact of the mass media, which portrays us as in narrowly defined, mostly negative and stereotypical ways.

During my teen years, I was hungry for information about Black culture and Black life. I devoured Essence, Ebony and Jet magazines. Eventually, I expanded my reading to include articles written about and by European writers. I regularly read about the exploits of young women in American society from the perspectives of the authors at Seventeen, Ms., Cosmopolitan, and Vogue magazines. In those publications, they described their notions of what women want, what happens to women in the workplace and in their marriages. Clearly, there was a working assumption, however limited and somewhat faulty, that what happened to White women was a universal experience because Black women's experiences were not referenced or included in those discussions. By never mentioning us, we became invisible, unimportant and thus unempowered.

There are some very compelling works that I have read that helped me to understand a great deal about the psychological images, cultural history and oppression of Black women in America. One was written by Carolyn West and is called, "Mammy, Sapphire and Jezebel: Historical Images of Black Women and Their Implications for Psychotherapy, 1995. A second was called, "The War Against Women" by Marilyn French, 1994. This book helped me to understand that women are oppressed all over the world, not just Black women. A third book that impressed me greatly was "When & Where I Enter: The Impact of Black Women on Race and Sex in America by Paula Giddings, 1996. Collectively, I learned that my experience as a Black woman was a shared experience with different time periods and players but with similar themes and objectives. A fourth book was called "Sister Citizen: Shame, Stereotypes and Black Women in America" by Melissa Harris Perry, 2013. Each of these books contain teachings on the history women and how their role, gender and identity as women have been shaped by political, economic, and sexual events across time.

### "Young Lady"

I will refer to my period of development as a young lady as the timeframe that begins with my college years. When I was graduating from Lindblom Technical College Preparatory High School in Chicago, I had very little inside knowledge as to where to go to college. Both my parents had attended college but never graduated with a degree. I think they thought that because I was a good student, I knew what I should do. I did not. My memory of that time period involves me using my woman's intuition to make the decision. I went to the college that offered me a scholarship, called me regularly, came to my high school to see me and arranged for me to visit their campus. In other words, I went where I thought I was most wanted. My school of choice at the time was 99% white-Manchester College, now Manchester University. Remember, I strongly identified as a "Black girl".

I had never really left the south side of Chicago, except for occasional trips to my grandmother's house in Mississippi. But when I went to my college of choice in Indiana, I liked it because it was different from Chicago. People looked you in the eye, spoke to you warmly and knew your name. I think I felt like I belonged there in spite of the obvious cultural differences of the majority population.

Yes. I experienced racism there but many other people tried to be genuinely warm and supportive because it was a church affiliated institution, Church of the Brethren to be exact. I cannot summarize all that I experienced as a young woman at Manchester College, but in short, I learned even more about who and what I was. Instead of learning this by assimilation, as I had done in Chicago. I learned by contrast. I was a different Black girl than the one portrayed on television on such shows as "The Jefferson's and Good Times". And I was certainly not the prostitute, drug addict or sex fiend portrayed in the Black exploitation films of the 70's and 80's.

During my years at Manchester, my learning and development was further expanded. I learned about "white folks," Indiana, farm life, the Church of the Brethren, the advantage of having a Black community and I learned about loving brothers. If I included my life of loving Black men, I would need way more than the pages allotted in this space and time. So I have chosen to focus my remaining thoughts on what I learned about my professional discipline, counseling psychology.

Through this educational journey, I learned to experience my feelings even more boldly, deeply, and completely. How? I had a very learned and esteemed professor who tutored me as an emerging professional psychologist/ counselor. As an undergraduate, I co-taught classes, wrote research papers, practiced my beginning counseling skills and blossomed as a leader among my professional peers. He and his wife introduced me to Re-evaluation Counseling. In essence, you talk about and re-experience every emotional hurt you have ever had and allow yourself to have cathartic expressions about the experiences. After your emotional discharge, you re-evaluate the experience with a renewed since of cognitive clarity. I spent years teaching and practicing this technique. It allowed me to "clean out and unlearn a great deal of misinformation and psychologically distressing events that occurred before and during my transition to graduate school.

The most important thing that I learned during my college years was how to love, forgive and lead. During my thirty plus years of studying and working in higher education, I have taken on the monumental task of helping other young women and men, especially of African descent, learn how to acquire knowledge of how to heal, and how to become more physically and emotionally healthy. I would like to think that I have also helped hundreds of students, adults and others overcome some of their greatest obstacles to thriving such as fear, ignorance, hunger, victimization, poverty, etc.

I am still learning these life lessons today but I am now trying to include others on my journey of healing and helping through teaching, training and research. So at this point in my life, I know how to learn. More importantly, I know how to unlearn negative experiences. Have I shared everything about what it feels like to be a Black woman? No. I have not. My experiences do not constitute the "universal" experience of Black womanhood. In fact, there is no one life that embodies the life of a Black woman. Together we have encountered the wrath of a nation, and together we can conquer all things that challenge us, limit us and attempt to define us. Our struggle is not over and neither is my journey...

# Chapter Twelve

## I Am Who I Am

*"Never underestimate the power of dreams and the influence of the human spirit. We are all the same in this notion: The potential for greatness lives within each of us." – Wilma Rudolph*

### JustDorcas AKA – Dorcas Wiley

When most of the world see me, I am Black first, then a woman. That's just the way it has been…no matter what is said or how wide the smile is… I am Black first…then a woman. And for me that is just fine! I do not mind being Black first, because I like my Blackness. The bigger part of it all is, after getting past me being Black first, then a women…then you get to meet me… Just Dorcas. Just Dorcas with the tight curly hair, the big thighs, thick lips and the dark chocolate brown skin tone…and I like my curly hair, my big thighs, thick lips and chocolate brown skin tone. Because that's a part of me and those beauty traits make me…me.

Has it always been easy and fun being seen Black first? No ma'am and no sir! There have been several challenges for me in being seen as Black first. I remember when I was young, about five or six years old, while sitting in my parents car with my daddy, waiting for momma to come out from shopping. I remember hearing this little White girl, who was sitting in the car next to us, ask her parent, "why is that man dirty?" referring to my daddy…a Black man. I don't remember much about the answer or reaction. I do remember daddy giving a little laugh. That's about all the reaction I remember. What stood out to me the most in that situation was the question, "why is that man dirty?" That was my first experience of someone seeing Black first.

I am a PK, (preacher's kid), and daddy preached at one of the few integrated congregations around at that time. A Church of Christ in Lansing Michigan. I was very young then and really do not remember much about that experience. I was seeing that experience through the eyes of a child, and being Black first wasn't something that affected me then. I didn't really know I was Black first… I just remember everyone being nice.

Life danced along for me, going to and from different states as dad preached at various congregations. I ended up graduating from a wonderfully mixed high school (Peach County High School in Fort Valley, GA) and was accepted into a majority White college (David Lipscomb College, now University, Nashville TN). High school was no real challenge, we were all Peach County High School Trojans and I have nothing but fond memories of my high school experience.

What do I remember about Lipscomb and being seen as Black first? I remember my speech professor, Dr. Connelly, teaching a class on voice inflection, asked me "Dorcas, how would a Black man say this?" to which I replied, " I do not know, I'm not a Black man." Challenges like those sprinkled throughout my college experience, but not enough to hinder or scar me. Life started to tumbled in. I had to start working. Most of my jobs were in corporate America. As I applied for jobs and completed applications, I was considered a double minority, because I was Black and a woman. Which, from my Human Resources experience, was a good thing because I filled two hiring requirements for the company. I should be valued. However, that wasn't the case. I was not viewed as a valued employee first. I was still viewed as Black, first.

Now, when most of the world sees me, I am a Black, college educated, working in corporate America, woman. Then I got married… now I am a Black, college educated, working in corporate America woman, who is a wife, next a mother and over it all a Christian. And to me… that's the way they viewed me. Always Black first then the rest in that order, without much weight on either.

I decided that I was going to be the best at being a Christian woman first, then the rest would fall in order. Now, that doesn't mean I didn't have to work at it, and it didn't mean that things were to fall in perfect order either. Things didn't magically fall in the perfect place because I was a Christian. By no means. There were times when things were said to me, that would not have been said to the other people that were seen, as "women" first. Things that could easily show the "hood" in some folks, moreover, I would always step back and put the "Christian woman" first. I would gracefully put them in their places, then K.I.M (keep it moving).

You see, you can do that without cussin', pointing your finger up in the air and slangin' your neck. You can do that in such a pleasant way, that they will not know what happened until they've processed the conversation seconds later. Then you walk away, leaving them with their mouth hanging open, high fiving' yourself in your mind, and K.I.M (keep it moving)!

Being in management positions in most of my places of employment just meant that I always had to walk taller, speak clearer, dress better and always have my stuff together. One of my managers stated during a performance review that I never stayed after hours to work. I immediately asked, "Is my work suffering? Am I not getting something done during normal working hours, that's making my performance suffer?" To that question he answered, with a chuckle, "well, no. I guess there is really no reason for you to stay late, is there?" You see he was looking for a reason to reprimand me during a performance review. He was searching for areas of improvement. With my question to his concern, that search ended. Then there were the promotions. Working in Human Resources and in banking, I was promoted to Lead Generalist providing HR support to a section of the Operations Department. There was another employee, one that didn't look anything like me, didn't get that promotion. She was visibly upset, cried and had to go home for the rest of the day. Then what happened? The next day, she got promoted to the same position I was promoted to.

Meaning we had to share the same position. Now there are two generalists supporting the same department (which wasn't needed). A few months later, guess who got laid off? Yours truly. Was it right? Was I mad? It doesn't matter. That's the way it was played out and I was comfortable with me. So I kept it moving. Working in corporate America and being Black first, then a woman, had many challenges, but nothing to hinder me from being me or scaring me for life.

As a Black woman, I felt I always had to work on keeping my stuff together....I had to. I had to work on having my personal relationship with God to help me deal with the various challenges. I worked on obtaining employment positions to build my resume and not just getting any ol' job. I had to work on being a happy wife and supporting a happy husband. I was a mother of three and had to work on developing well rounded children who all were different and all had various challenges as well…but again, nothing to hinder me from being me…I had to handle all aspects of my life. I had to have my stuff together and still smile, even when I didn't feel like smiling…I smiled. That's what we do… as Black women; we always have to our stuff together and we keep smiling…. right?

I didn't do this alone, by any means. My mother was my role model. She, being a preacher's wife and moving from state to state, had to keep it together and it wasn't easy. Looking back, I can see how hard it was. Trying to keep her preacher husband happy, healthy and well fed. Being a stay at home mother, for the most part, and raising three children. I couldn't see it then, but looking back, it wasn't so easy because she was also seen as Black first, then the wife of the preacher, then the mother of three children, then Mable. But I never saw her falter, or fall. I remember some difficult times in our family.

I remember mom almost miscarrying her last child, my younger brother. I saw her leaving the house quietly crying and coming back smiling (because all was well). She knew how to surrender it all to God long before I understood the full concept of "surrendering." Thanks to mom, Mable Juanita Wiley, for being my Black female role model to assist me in my journey.

Then life tossed me, as a Black woman, some really big personal challenging opportunities. Those challenging opportunities were, being twice divorced, twice laid-off within two years, and then the big BC - Breast

Cancer. But this wasn't supposed to happen to me, because, you see, I had my stuff together.

My dad was a preacher. I'm a preacher's daughter. We went to church every Sunday morning and Sunday evening. I went to the gospel meetings, the week long kind. I was baptized at an early age. My relationship with God was a serious one. I remember my older siblings teasingly call me "Holy Woman" when I was a child. I really wanted to (and still do) please God, and go to heaven at the judgment. Those challenging opportunities were not supposed to happen to me, because I was a good Christian girl, who grew into a good Christian woman, who happened to be Black. I wasn't promiscuous. I did not drink, smoke, use illegal drugs or abuse my body. I worked smart and I worked hard. I was a good wife and a good mother. These things were not supposed to happen to me.

So why were these challenges so heavy in my life? So heavy that they were making me physically, mentally and emotionally sick. I knew I could not go on like that, and I realized that I needed to learn how to release things in order to move forward – which is another thing we, as Black women, very seldom do. We seldom release things because we are supposed to have it all together and are expected to handle it all … and handle it well. But, I had to learn how to release things in order to move forward.

Well, I was still here. Still facing so many heavy burdens. The preacher's daughter, twice divorced, with three children. I will not go into the details of the divorces, because that is not what is important now. What is important is how I handled it, and how I didn't allow it to handle me. It was during this time that I cried and didn't understand why these specific things were happening to me. Concerning my marriages, I didn't know what I did wrong or what more I could have done before and during the marriages. One thing for sure, I did learn what to do after them, and that was to surrender all to God.

I did not want divorce in my life. I did not want to be added to the Black divorced single parent statistic list. I did not want to be another single Black parent in America. My parents have been married for over 60 years and this is what I wanted for my life. I had children, I did not want this for them, but life had a different plan for me. It is still hard for me to say, but yes, I am a single Black mom who has been divorced….twice!

Then there were the layoffs from jobs that I really enjoyed. One came with plenty of warning and the other came with the door - knob hitting me where…(as the ol' folks say) the good Lord…well …you know the rest. The government job gave me a "thrown together" going away party. But the female White girl who left before me, and had not been there as long as I had, got a well planned party, with many state and other agencies people invited. She had Food galore, cute little finger sandwiches, gherkin pickles, peanuts, mints, cake and cookies. Me…I got a cake, and those who happened to be around at the time, were invited to the "kick'er out" party. But please keep in mind…I still was comfortable with me being who I am… with or without that grand going away party and with or without that government job.

It was hard when I was laid off from my places of employment. Both times, I was a single parent, and felt like I really had no one that I could lean on to help me during this, (what I felt like), devastating time in my life, at least no one here on earth. I guess the main reason I was feeling that way was because, as I said earlier, as a Black woman, I was supposed to have it altogether, keep smiling, and certainly not tell anyone that I was having problems.

One thing for sure is most Black women carry a strong faith in God and I was no exception. I knew God helped me, each time, because I can honestly say, I never wanted for anything I needed. So I had to get it together. I had to get my mind right. I wasn't going to stop living. I was not going to crumble and die because of the losses. My life will go on, life must go on. I have learned that there are blessings in everything; you just have to look for them.

With my first job loss, the blessing was that I was able to spend the summer with my children for the first time in their lives. With my second job loss the blessing was finding that I had cancer. You see, if I had not gotten laid off in December 2009 and was not in the position of losing my health insurance at the end of the month, I probably would not have gone for a physical. If I had not gotten a physical and a mammogram (suggested by my GYN), I would not have known I had stage 1 breast cancer one month later. This, coupled with everything else I never expected in my life and did not see coming, seemed to rip out a part of my soul. Simply rip the insides of my soul completely out. All are things from time to time; that put me, as a woman that was Black, in stressful places. Yet, as Maya Angelou said, "I Rise."

I was stressed. I was a single Christian mother, who happened to be Black and I was stressed. So, what did I do? I surrendered! I recognized and admitted that this stuff was bigger than me and I surrendered…to my higher being…to God.

I shared my situation with those around me, those who loved me. I had a group of friends I called my "posse" and they had my back. Men, but mostly women. Majority Black women and this was a great example of Black women sticking together. Black women really need to learn to stick together. Learn to really have each other's back and lift each other up. Stop calling each other b's and hoe's (by the way the correct word is spelled whores and pronounced as such). We chant "Black Lives Matter!" However, I want us to fully understand that Black lives will never matter until it matters to US! Until we stop acting like crabs in a barrel, trying to pull others down so we can be on top.

We are going to be challenged with many opportunities in our life. I have only shared a bit of my life. I got a whole bunch more that you may be able to relate to, but for now, let's just say; the best way to inspire you is to tell you what I did to inspire me. I learned how to surrender and that is not easy. I also decided I mattered. I decided that I was a Christian first, then a woman who happened to be Black. I decided that being seen as "Black first" was a reality and it was okay with me, because I know! I decided that I love my curly hair; my big thighs, my thick lips and I love my chocolate brown skin tone.

All in all, I remember I am a child of God. I remember this is the same God that feeds and watches over the birds of the air and the lilies of the fields. I know, that this same God loves me. Sure I get tired, sure I cry and get angry at the situations and sometimes I simply do not understand why. But I know I am His child and if I surrender all to Him things will eventually work out.

Sometimes we have to find our higher power. It may be the same God I honor. It may be something else for you… it may be, you. Whatever that power is, make sure it is a positive power to help you grow. Know that your life matters… you matter. We come in all shapes, sizes and hues, and we all matter. Make sure you stand stronger, stand taller…and RISE.

# Reflections from the Soul

# Chapter Thirteen

## Black Marriages Matter

*"Nothing will work unless you do." – Maya Angelou*

### Justice and Somone

Finding the special someone, planning the special day, repeating the nuptial vows and riding off in marital bliss is a fairy tale part of the "American Dream" that every girl or woman hopes and dreams for. But the unity of marriage encompasses much more than capturing each other; it is a covenant, not a contract, but a bond, a comprehensive and permanent commitment between a man and woman who love each other.

I met Justice 20 years ago in the bookstore on the campus of the university both he and I attended. It is so vivid in my mind. I had gone into the bookstore between classes. The jewelry caught my eye – I really like jewelry. I picked up different items, earrings, chains and necklaces. Each time I picked up an item and was about to return it, the turn-about moved, I turned it back around, returned the item, picked up another piece, looked at it, ready to return it, and again, the turn-about had moved. I picked up another piece and the same thing happened again. I looked up and he was standing there laughing at me, in amazement. I started to smile and then he said, "I am Justice" and I said, "Hi, I am Somone." From there, we exchanged all our vital information, my campus address and his home address. He was a native and still lived at home with his parents' in the city. Needless to say, the very next morning Justice called to ask me to meet him at the band room; being a music major he was there all day. I agreed. Later that day during my lunch break, I met him and he handed me a box and inside was a silver chain I had looked at the previous day. We had lunch and we both enjoyed the conversation. This became the beginning of many great days ahead.

We began to date. I would go out to his parents' house or he would pick me up and we would ride the city, listen to music, talk, laugh, and enjoy each other. We enjoyed each other, we fit together like a glove, and we had so much fun.

We were comfortable with each other – it was like we had known each other for a lifetime. You know, you can meet someone and instantly know this is someone you want to know more; you can feel their soul and it is great. We started to explore our lives together. We went to Church together, family gatherings, discussed our future desires, children, finances, even retirement. The communication was great; the relationship grew. He was affectionate, he made me feel safe and we fell in love.

Justice and I graduated in the Spring of 1992. He landed a position as band director at the University of Louisville in Kentucky and I was returning to my hometown to teach English at my high school Alma Mater. The day I moved out of my dorm, Justice came over to help me. He had a solemn look on his face; we were both leaving. I asked him what was wrong? I could see tears in his eyes, which only made me teary as well. As I picked up the last box to set on top of the others, I turned around and there was an open Black box sitting on top of the packed boxes; a ring, a small but nice diamond ring. He got on his knees and asked the magical question, "Will you marry me?" The immediate response was, "Yes."

A smile as big as the Grinch came over my face, my heart filled with happiness and I was the happiest woman in the world. I was engaged to be married, not just married, but married to a loving, sweet, affectionate and caring man who wanted to take me over the threshold of holy matrimony to love and to cherish 'til death do us part. I was going to belong to someone and we were going to become one.

We had a quick but small wedding at my home church on June 10th of that year and traveled to Kentucky to start our new life together. He started working immediately, preparing for his new career. In the fall, I began working as an English teacher at the local high school, not far from the university. We were both happy. We had very little money, but we both knew we wanted to be successful in life together. We wanted to be able to buy a home and raise a family together. We looked at both of our incomes and pooled our monies together in one bank account. We both had old cars that our parents had given us while in college, and we only lived about 10 minutes away from work, which helped us stay within our budget. After paying our bills, we had just enough money to travel back and forth to work, but we created a budget and lived by it. We took our lunch to work, our bills were paid, we had gas money, air and heat, clothes to wear and, most of all, we had each other. We lived a simple life, but a happy, fulfilled one.

Justice was very busy during the Fall with marching band and concert band in the Winter. I would travel with him on the weekends. It was our time together, even though he was working. The band students would always say, Mr. and Mrs. Carson need their time together and we would find our special spot for the two of us. We had a beautiful marriage. We loved God and we loved each other. We put God first in our life, we served him and we prayed together. We lived a moral life together, we believed in the power and the unity of marriage and we kept our vows sacred.

We had a great understanding and we respected each other. Someone told me once, that it is a foolish woman who disrespects her man and a great way to lose him if you did not. A man wants to be respected, as a woman wants to be loved and Justice loved me and I respected him as the man.

We believed to have a great marriage. We needed to keep it alive and continue some of the same activities we had prior to marriage. I firmly believe that men don't want their wife to change after marriage and women make the mistake of trying to change their husband once they are married. If we practice not changing and not trying to change the man, it is one less battle to fight.

Justice was a very affectionate man and playful as well. He could turn a heated moment into a laughing one and sometimes I wondered, what was the issue? He sent me flowers for a very special reason – he loved me. And I returned the affection. I would leave him notes on the counter top or under his pillow or drop rose petals on the floor from the door to the bedroom to let him know I was waiting for him. We held on to each other, we hugged and kissed, and held hands when we were together.

Many times we sat in front of the fireplace to eat or just as a way to cozy up. If anyone knows the power of love, hold on to a person's hand. It is the most romantic and powerful gesture a man can show a woman – real intimacy and secureness.

Justice worked long hours and I greeted him with open arms, and praised him for being a great provider and he praised me for being his soul mate and an awesome wife. Showing affection to your spouse helps when you have had a bad day at work, when your feet hurt or when things are not going well in the world. Knowing you have a wonderful and understanding spouse to come home to makes all the difference in the world. It helps you to go out the next day to conquer the world and to "slay the giant like David in the bible," if you have to; so when I greeted him at the door with a big hug and kiss and threw my long legs around his waist, he could only succumb. Sure we had arguments, however, they were for the moment but not monumental.

We agreed to argue fairly, to discuss the issues at hand and never put each other down, curse and never go to bed at night without saying "good night." I must add the make-up was always worth it.

We promised we would never argue about each other's family, anything we needed to say, we said it with tact. We both had great relationships with our in-laws', however we stayed a distance from them so we both welcomed them when they visited. I firmly believe that if parents like your spouse and respect them; it helps the marriage.

I always knew I was safe with him and he always knew when I needed my emotions stroked and when I needed physical intimacy. We both were aware of that; that's how in tuned we were to each other. I will never forget, the advice my grandmother gave me before Justice and I got married, and that was to never punish your husband by withholding sex from him. She said that is a big mistake because if you don't, someone else will. And I never did. We were both sexual beings and we enjoyed one another. We kept our sex life invigorating and fun. We explored each other's body and knew the right things to do and trying something different and in different places add spice to lovemaking. We enjoyed each other.

After five years together, Joshua and I had saved enough money that we could purchase our dream home. We were fortunate enough to replace our cars and we were living a lavish life. We decided that we were ready to start our family. We were not in a hurry but we were ready to embark on the next level of our life. We continued our usual intimate activities but we never got pregnant. At first, we were not too concerned due to the fact I had been on birth control for years. So we continued, and month after month, still no pregnancy.

Then it came time for my annual medical physical and mammogram. After my first mammogram there was a suspicious spot in my breast and I was called back for an ultrasound to determine whether it was a cyst or a solid mass. The prognosis was in. It was a solid mass. It seemed my happy life had made a 180 degree turn. Justice and I had many questions and concerns, but we faced our challenges like champs and did not hesitate. We were fighters and we had each other.

From that point, I was scheduled for a breast biopsy. Tissue from the breast was removed to check for cancerous cells. The results were positive; I had breast cancer. The entire time I went through these procedures, my husband was with me. He provided me with emotional support. He was inspirational. He gave me pep talks. He held me. He kissed me. And he held my hand throughout the entire process. He assured me, he would be with me through every step. Justice let me know that he and I were alright, that our marriage, faith, and love was solid enough to face any obstacle that life threw at us. Justice made sure he was at every appointment with me. We got second opinions and he researched any tests or procedures I was recommended to take before it was scheduled. When I cried, he cried, when I laughed, he laughed, when I hurt, he hurt; he was my rock throughout all of this. We knew the days ahead would not be easy.

He took a leave of absence from work when I had my full breast mastectomy, radiation, and transplant. I had pretty long hair – honey blonde hair. We both did not want it ruined by the radiation therapy, so Justice cut it for me and shaved my head. I remember that day. He had tears in his eyes as he cut each section. In honor of me, he shaved his and kept it shaved throughout the process. He sat with me, held my hand and prayed for me. He waited on me from head to toe; he never left my side. He made sure I was confident about my body – that I was loved and we were secure in our relationship.

We joined a support group for couples and one each for the survivor. He joined one for the care-giver for spouse or partner. We survived it together. Throughout our relationship, we spent time together, we learned each other, we communicated, we shared some of the same interest and values, we were able to be our own individual self and we never put each other down for our differences. We expected respect and we gave respect.

We honored each other and our faith was as one. We were each other's friend and soul mate. Having cancer brought us closer together, helped us to value each other more and our faith grew stronger. These qualities are not found in every marriage. We knew we had built a solid foundation and together we could conquer the world. We didn't know what the future held but we knew we would conquer it together.

As I look at so many marriages that do not have the basis – the solid foundation to stay in a marriage when trouble comes – I realize that Justice and I are truly blessed to have each other. We may not have the opportunity for our little replicas to run around and to share some of the love that we have, but we have each other.

I am blessed to be a Black woman married to a Black man. We need to give our Black men moral support, lift him up, praise and celebrate him, respect him, and love him. Society has shut our Black men out. They are missing in action because of societal issues. The job market has fallen, the increase of imprisonment, drug use and discrimination and put-downs among our Black men has taken away their value. The Black race is almost extinct and the culture and values of the Black man is almost non-existent.

We must do something about our most valued and prized possessions. In return, our Black men can love the Black woman, respect, love and cherish them and together we can conquer the world.

It is unfortunate that the appearance of breast cancer forced my husband to have a deep sense of introspection, which made him more attentive to me. Nevertheless, it inspired him to love me unconditionally. I am honored, inspired, and thankful that our love and commitment has been renewed.

What is the purpose of "tying the knot," the convent called marriage and what does it really mean to the Black race? The Black marriage is a part of our history and has "stood the test of time." We are survivors of marriage, it is us, it is in us as Black people to be married. Marriage is an enriched part of our culture. Our ancestors survived unthinkable stresses and challenges to be married and to raise their family.

The trials, tribulations, and hardships that the Black race endured to be married and to save their family brings about strength, fortitude and courage to us and should give the Black race encouragement and determination to survive our marriages of today. We come from generations of marriages – the bond that brings us together, to stay together, to pull our resources to become a strong unit.

What can we learn from our ancestors? We can learn that the hardships and problems that our ancestors experienced are monumental to those that couples deal with today and survived. They were committed to their claim, not the contract but a covenant, the comprehensive and permanent commitment between a man and a woman.

# Chapter Fourteen

Angry Black Woman

*"The triumph can't be had without the struggle."*
*– Wilma Rudolph*

### K. Dawn Rutledge

I am an angry Black woman.
There.
I said it.
And now my question is, 'what's wrong with that?!'
This is a natural emotion, and everybody experiences it every once and awhile. But, for some reason, when the label is attached to a Black woman, its connotation becomes this red-eyed bull who cannot be tamed by the matador.

I find that anger is not always about a bad attitude. Oftentimes it represents hurt, pain, disappointment, discrimination, fear, rejection and a host of other challenges unique to the Black woman's experience. In many instances, it is a cry for help.

There are times when we use our anger to lash out, but over the years, I have learned to use it to educate, protect and prepare myself. It is not an anger of hate or meanness, but one of guarded awareness.

My story is no more fascinating than that of many Black women. But it is mine. The lessons I have learned throughout my life are valuable enough that they could help someone to avoid similar pitfalls or maybe even relatable enough that those women who have found themselves in similar situations can unearth a sisterhood of support and empowerment, of which I am a huge proponent.

As a young girl, I grew up with what most every child needs – food, clothing, shelter, love, and discipline, when necessary. I was blessed to grow up around and be mentored and supported by so many awesomely talented and powerful Black women. The older I got, I continued to befriend women who fell into that same category.

Unlike the environment that young Black girls are exposed to today, I grew up relatively green. There were no social media influences or unflattering images of women taunting me to want to look, behave or talk a certain way. Now, don't get me wrong, as an MTV-generation kid, there were plenty of things that began to shape my thinking, but certainly nothing as in-your-face as what young people have exposure to today.

I was raised to be a decent person; to have respect for myself and others; to carry myself with dignity and class; to use my intelligence. I was raised that I am not better than anyone else, but not to stoop down to gutter levels. To be an independent thinker, to not let people run over me, to be my best.

So, why am I so angry? One simple answer: life. My grandmother always used to say, "just keep living." I know what that means now.

As a child, there's so much that does not faze us. We don't have the same worry of grown-ups...that is until we grow up. I think I discovered my first real anger as a teenager. I had a crush on this guy who did not quite feel the same about me. He was older than me and he liked another girl. A White girl. This is a rejection that many Black women are hurt by. I don't know why but it just makes us feel devalued...well, it made me feel that way. I was pissed. How could he like her over me? She wasn't even as cute as I was. This may not have been the root of my anger, but it certainly helped to precipitate it.

It wasn't long before I graduated from high school and had my sights set on college. A fresh start is sometimes vital. I left what I was familiar with for something completely foreign to me. No family. No friends. It was during college that I really began to discover myself and all those lessons learned as a child began to come full circle. I got involved in several organizations, made lifelong friends and began preparing myself for a career that I still love to this day. But college was not without its challenges, too. It was the first time in my life that I experienced real loss. My paternal grandmother passed away, and it became difficult for me to accept morality. In my grief, I felt sadness, then hurt and anger – an emotion becoming all-too-familiar to me. But like all things, this too shall pass.

After college, I started my career, got married and eventually had a child. I was married for a good while until it just wasn't working anymore. That can make you angry. No one gets married with the thought of divorce. You always expect a happily-ever-after. A long life together – not without its ups and downs – that would not be realistic – but certainly one that you could look back on and see more good than bad. One that would create amazing memories that realize the hopes and dreams you have for your children and grandchildren. But that did not happen for me. Divorce is ugly. It is painful. It's sad. It's angry. It hurts, just another contributor to the mad Black woman persona.

One of the most eye-opening experiences in my life came from my career. The challenges of working in business and corporate settings can be tough. Throughout my career, I have had both male and female bosses, Black and White. As a Black woman, you constantly struggle to find the right balance. If you are too cautious, you could be labeled as not contributing enough. If you are too outspoken, you are being disrespectful or militant. If you are too aggressive, well, you may have heard the term used for a female dog. While on the surface a cautious yet outspoken and aggressive leader sounds like an ideal addition to any team, but not so much for Black women.

I think many of us know the playing field is not always fair, particularly working in majority environments, but when your own people stab you – that is a disappointment and hurt like none other. I experienced it firsthand. It feels like someone who you thought would extend you a hug, instead comes up and punches you in the gut. It makes you angry. Or, at least, it made me angry. The professional sabotage, the disrespect, underhanded dealings, lies and, even taking credit for my work, added to my rage…all crimes committed toward me by another Black woman. The irony! You spend time wondering how a sister could do that to another sister and be okay with it. I may not like you, but I am certainly not going to sabotage you.

I am not going to jeopardize your livelihood. I'm not going to purposely try to ruin your career. But what I learned in this situation is that for some people, it's all about them. It is sad, but true. Loyalty means nothing. Honesty means nothing. Fairness means nothing. Support means nothing. Respect means nothing. I also learned what I am made of – resilience, strength, gifted, intelligent, anointed – and can't be stopped.

The interesting thing about the emotion of anger is that like all other human emotions, there are lessons to learn from its experience. And as author Iyanla Vanzant would say, "if you do the work," you come out on the other side better, stronger, wiser and more joyful about what you have learned and how it can be applied to your life and your interactions with others.

I still get angry about things at times…like the mistreatment of people, disrespect, or even poor grades on my son's report card. What can I say? I am human. I do not buy into the myth that there is something wrong with being an angry Black woman. It is a natural emotion, and with all emotions that we experience, it is about our attitudes and behaviors – both of which we have complete control over. Anger can be empowering and educational. We learn by living.

Look, when I get angry, do not expect me to start throwing things and making a spectacle of myself. You might receive a few choice words, though (smile). There is no question that anger can creep in when least expected circumstances stir it up. But what I have learned, as I have matured and as I have experienced different things in my life, is you must own your part in whatever it is…and there is always something that you can own. Regardless of the who, what and why of the anger, I can handle it. I refuse to dumb myself down for anyone. I'm smart and good at what I do. I own that blessing and all that comes with it.

I am reminded and empowered by words written by spiritual teacher and author Marianne Williamson. In her book, <u>A Return to Love: Reflections on the Principles of a Miracle</u>, she inspires us to reflect on how truly powerful we all are. I believe this is especially relevant for many Black women to take to heart considering the feelings of inadequacy, fear, sadness and anger we often experience:

*"Our deepest fear is not that we are inadequate. Our deepest fear is that we are powerful beyond measure. It is our light, not our darkness that most frightens us. We ask ourselves, Who am I to be brilliant, gorgeous, talented, fabulous? Actually, who are you not to be? You are a child of God. Your playing small does not serve the world. There is nothing enlightened about shrinking so that other people won't feel insecure around you. We are all meant to shine, as children do. We were born to make manifest the glory of God that is within us. It's not just in some of us; it's in everyone. And as we let our own light shine, we unconsciously give other people permission to do the same. As we are liberated from our own fear, our presence automatically liberates others."*

Black women share common experiences and, in that, there is an obligation to do better for ourselves and for each other. There is an unspoken sisterhood, I believe. Where there are opportunities to mentor, support, encourage and educate one another, then we should do it. Tearing one another down doesn't make us better – it only exposes our insecurities.

There's no question that being a Black woman in America is one of the hardest positions on earth. Yet, time and time again, we have proven our ability to rise above the multitude of challenges we face with a strength that can only be explained as generationally - inherited and faith-filled. It is my hope that we will continue to lift as we climb, and that we will continue to show our appreciation for and celebrate those who come before us.

We must understand that there is nothing new under the sun; just a different day packaged within a different decade with new names and phrases. The generations who have come before us are just as important as those who will come behind us. And our realization must be that you can't have success today without acknowledging the contributions and sacrifices of those before us.

So when I hear the term "angry Black woman," I don't hang on to the derogatory connotation that some might want to attach to it. Angry is more than an emotion. It is a powerful action that can be tamed into empowerment. Yes, I will admit that some of my anger has led to petty disputes, avoidance, and an attitude, but you learn as you grow older that life is short, and being angry dampens your joy. That is why it's important to turn it into positive action. In other words, you control it. You do not let it control you.

Throughout history, I have learned about Black women who got angry, but made a positive difference. These women took that anger and turned it into action for the betterment of all our lives. Women like Harriet Tubman who got angry about the inhumane conditions of slavery which led to the creation of the Underground Railroad, at the time, one of the most sophisticated networks designed to help escaped slaves to freedom. And Ida B. Wells who bravely documented the tragic practice of the lynching of Black people in the United States in local newspapers.

Then I proudly remember the stand taken by Rosa Parks, whose tired feet prompted her to continue sitting in a bus seat designated for Whites, and led to the rise of the Montgomery Boycott. Or the tenacity of Shirley Chisholm, an educator turned politician, who refused to accept the status quo and became the first African-American woman elected to Congress and, ultimately, the first Black and first woman candidate to run for a major party's nomination for President of the United States.

So, if I can emulate the work of these dynamic women, feel free to call me an angry Black woman. Now, back to my original question: 'what's wrong with that?!'

# Chapter Fifteen

## The Chains are Broken

*"Black women in general need to know that it's OK for them to be the way they are — to see the way they are as a strength, and to be liberated from fear and from silence."*
— *Wangari Maathai*

### Willette Pare

I often ponder in my mind why I and others like me are often called, gay, butch, dike, lesbian, homosexual, funny, sick, tomboy, chap-stick, and bull-dagger. Sometimes, I wonder why I am the way I am, is it a genetic defect? There are people born with physical and mental disabilities, aren't they? It could be a genetic mishap, like being born without or with too many extremities. I wonder why people won't accept me? I wonder why I don't like bright colors? I wonder why it is an abomination to God? Aren't I his child as well, and aren't we all taught that he loves everyone?

Why can't I be who I want to be and be socially acceptable by others? Why are people so critical? These are the thoughts and questions running through my mind, thoughts that plague me, that keep me from living the life I truly want to live, the "normal" life as others. I am a lesbian. I have always known there was something different about me.

I am the youngest of three girls. The last child my mother and father had because of the many complications my mother endured with miscarriages and childbirth. We practically lost her to postpartum hemorrhage, a serious but rare condition that occurs after delivery. The doctors could not get her blood to clot after delivery. It was a touch and go situation and many women die as a result of this type of episode. My mother, father and children were blessed on that day.

Consequently, my parents decided that it wasn't worth the risk to try for a boy. My father was happy with his three girls and even happier that I wanted to hang out with him. My father's name is Willie and my parents named me Willette after they decided I would be their last, which left them with no other opportunities to have the boy my father desired.

As a small child, I was not the "Barbie Doll" girl unless we played house, and I was the father. The only thing I remember ever doing that resembled a female was wearing my mother's high-heel shoes. I think most children male or female at some point in time, wore their mother's shoes. That was okay, I guess at least for me.

I remember my male cousins loved to visit to hang out with my dad and one time they left some trucks and G.I. Joe male action figures at our house. I played with those, instead of the "girlie" toys. My older sisters would become very angry with me because I did not want to play with them or have sleep overs with my other female cousins.

My daddy was an outdoorsman. As a small child, my father dragged me with him everywhere. He taught me how to hunt, fish, build things, and play football, basketball, baseball and golf. My mother on the other hand, insisted that I wear a dress, frilly socks and shoes and ribbons in my hair, which I detested. I protested against wearing this type of apparel and my father agreed with me. I remember crying and saying that the dresses itched and my mother would change me into khaki pants and cotton tops.

Finally, she gave up. She was fighting a losing battle with both my father and me. My dad started shopping with me and allowed me to choose my own clothes. I chose cargo pants, khaki or black, buttoned shirts, plaids or stripes, and boots.

When my cousins visited, I played video games, football, and basketball with my male cousins. My father wanted me to play basketball and go to the WNBA. He played basketball all his life and was up for a draft when he tore his ACLs. He insisted I play basketball to fulfill his dream. He enrolled me into basketball camps and I played recreational ball, school ball, AAU ball, middle school and high school ball. I became a star player. I was the "chip off the old block," when it came to basketball. As I started to go through puberty, my hands and feet grew exceptionally large, larger than usual, like my Dad's. I remember feeling quite awkward and the girls and boys teased me about my extremely large hands and feet. I was so awkward that I would buy shoes smaller than I needed and that hurt. Even family members made derogatory statements about my size. My mother became worried because I never put on a dress. She made statements like; "Girls don't suppose to have a ball in their hand all the time." But I was happy, and my dad approved, that's all I needed.

In my middle school years, I was the star player for my team, scoring over 20 points, and 10-15 rebounds per game. I ran track, cross country, played volleyball and softball, I was all around a great athlete and received MVP in basketball. Middle school brought on new and different changes for me. I was attracted to girls, but I was afraid to approach them. I remember some girls smiling at me, however, I was uncertain of the meaning so I did not approach them. Other girls were not very accepting of me and quite honestly that was okay. The boys made their smart remarks and called me a "butch" or "dike." Those words were always offensive to me and I started to feel depressed about my whole life, except when I was with my dad.

We always seemed to connect. Although my mom was constantly on me, my dad was so happy he had someone in his image — he could not see the "forest for the trees." But as you grow older, you want to have your own friends and be accepted by your peers, but it wasn't happening. Eventually, I hooked up with some other outcasts in the school and started to drink and use drugs. As long as I was high and hanging out with someone other than my dad, I was happy. I noticed I was becoming more depressed and thought about suicide. I got my daddy's gun several times but I could not pull the trigger.

One night I went out with the gang and indulged heavily in alcohol, smoked marijuana and popped some pills. On my way home, I fell out and luckily some of my friends found me and I was rushed to the hospital. I recovered, but I still did not tell my parents what was going on. All they really knew was I was using drugs.

The next year I went to high school and that Fall, I made the basketball team. I don't think there was one true heterosexual girl on the squad. Some tried not to be, those were in questioning. I felt right at home, even though I had not officially owned my feelings and true identity.

Then one day it happened. I was in the shower and it seemed no one was there but me. This is the day I was "turned out." This was the day, my whole life changed. If I ever had any doubt, it became clear to me. I can imagine it was like any girls first time, although I was having sex with another girl. She "rocked my world." It was no more turning back for me.

Suddenly, the shower curtain flew open and it was Edwin (Edwina), she had been looking at me, giving me the eye since tryouts, but she had a girl. She stepped into the shower and she started to rub me on my breast, her lips pressed against mine, then she put her hand on my vagina and then her finger inside of me. It felt so good. Then she kneeled down and stuck her hard tongue onto my clitoris and began to stroke it – the strokes became faster and harder. It felt so good. From that point on, I knew there was no turning back. For once in my life, I felt whole and happy. We never stopped. We continued – we were a couple. But I knew there was more to this romance.

Now I needed to come out and be honest with my family, friends and school community, but who to talk to was a mystery to me and I was afraid. One day not long after that I noticed that my health teacher, Ms. Morris had an Ally sign in the window of her classroom door. I was standing there looking at it and she approached me. As I was about to ask, she stated, "Yes, I can talk to you." From that point, I felt relieved that I could finally say to someone, an adult, that I am gay. I remember she was so understanding and comforting to me.

She convinced me to tell my parents and family and assured me she would be there to support me. And she did, she helped me throughout the entire process. We set up a meeting time at home, and I told my parents. Both were hurt in the beginning and my mother blamed my dad and my dad blamed my mother and we cried. It wasn't long before they accepted me, because both reflected back on my life from the beginning and now they could accept who I was. Then I informed them I wanted to be called "Will," short for Willette.

My teacher helped me a great deal. Together we formed an Ally group at school and met on a regular basis. Ms. Morris was a life-saver for me and many of the students at school. She advocated for us and made sure we were heard. She provided professional development to the teachers and staff at school and then across the district. Now it has become a district-wide initiative and all new staff are required to complete the training when hired.

We held forums to educate other students, parents and the community about the LGBTQ (Lesbian, Gay, Bisexual, Transgender, and Questioning) community. The main things we needed people to know was that we were just like everyone else. We have feelings and we are human. We are talented and smart and we can be as successful as the next person. Signs and posters filled the walls of our school to let everyone know we were intricate to the school culture. Sure, some still had their negative comments, smirks and looks. We've come a long way and we've fought a good fight.

We held special rallies and educational sessions on suicide, depression, HIV/AIDS and sexually transmitted infections, bullying and drug prevention. LGBTQ (Lesbian, Gay, Bisexual, Transgender, Questioning) youth exhibit behaviors of sadness; depression, worthlessness, withdrawal and recklessness in their life because they have no one to talk to, because they are ridiculed, called names and made to feel they are less than human beings. LGBTQ youth attempt suicide at a rate 2-4 more times than heterosexual teens and their attempts are more serious, higher attempt to die and methods more lethal. LGBTQ youth are stressed from (distal) discrimination, prejudices and rejection results in proximal stressors, feeling the need to conceal their true identity, having intrusive thoughts about their secret, becomes isolated and withdrawn from their family, friends and community, and suffer from shame and guilt. (youthprideri.org) This was so important to me as a LGBTQ youth growing up and finally receiving the support of my family and school made the transition to becoming a free person to say, "Yes, I am a lesbian."

I never felt awkward ever again. My life and others' lives were saved – we were free to be who we really were born to be. I completed high school and received a scholarship to play basketball at a Division 1A University. I settled in during the summer for basketball practice and felt comfortable as I was accepted by my teammates.

Immediately, I knew that most of the players were like me, and those who were not, accepted me. During the Fall, I joined the campus LGBTQ organization and became an Ally and I chose to major in anthropology, focusing on sociocultural anthropology. My desire was to help other students who were open, those who were not open yet and those still in the questioning stage.

I wanted to help the Black students because being a Black female and homosexual can be overwhelming. I wanted the LGBTQ students to know they had a strong support system, although some were accepting, there were still others that were homophobic. Being LGBTQ, we are subject to bullying, discrimination and harassment at a totally different level than anyone else and I knew I could help change the stigma of the LGBTQ community.

Being a Black person in general, we endure a certain level of hate and to add homosexuality to the equation, only escalates the hate factor. However, hate for homosexuality is not just a racial issue but religion is a major factor especially among the Black American. The Black community will quickly say, a gay person is possessed by the devil and create a "war room," to pray away the evil spirit. Being Black and LGBTQ, in the Black community is a cause of being scorned—you can lose your family, culture, community and the bottom line rejection. I had a friend whose father blatantly told his daughter until she changed her mind-set, that she was not related to him.

Homophobia has gender barriers as well. Men in general look at two lesbian women differently than two gay men. Gay men are looked upon as disgusting and some straight men have no desire to be near a gay man, however two lesbian women are considered sexually attractive. Some straight men won't allow their sons to say words they deem"girlie" like "cute." They may not allow their sons to play with boys who may not be "rough and tough," or to cry when hurt, for fear they may be encouraging feminine tendencies.

I was once asked by a Black male to allow him to watch Edwin and I make love to each other. It infuriated me. I take the same respect and privacy for Edwin and I as I would if I was with a man. My love life is private, as should the heterosexual couple. I think when Black men think of two women together, it is more of a sexual fantasy for them, rather than two women who are truly in love with each other and who have a healthy, loving relationship.

When will the LGBTQ community be accepted among the Black community or in society as a whole? Homosexuality is a part of our history. It has been recorded that the first Black homosexual woman would be 189 years old today. In the history of our country, the LGBTQ community has a history of iconic successes and talents ranging from grandiose artists to ones who have influenced the foreign diplomats. It is the time for acceptance. The younger generation will accept the LGBTQ community more readily as it becomes a part of their norm versus the older adult who is still stuck in the sand where homosexuality is concerned.

It is time that the Black community and our country recognize and accept the LGBTQ community; we are not going anywhere, and we are not going to change because someone wants us to. Our communities are suffering from pure ignorance. We need to have open conversations about it, to find ways to accept it, to accept that we are human; we have feelings and we are a viable part of society.

We eat and breathe as everyone else. Being homophobic can destroy our country, communities, family and society as a whole. We are driven by fear and fear brings on uncertainty, and the lack of growth keeps us stagnant. To move our communities, we need more education on the LGBTQ community to unleash the fear.

What does it mean to be a Black woman, who is a lesbian? It means that I love me. I love my Blackness, I love that I love a Black woman. I have strong convictions for Black lives and Black rights. Yes, I fight battles. I fight the same battles as the heterosexual Black woman in society, as being overlooked in the White American workplace. Am I invisible? Yes I am, I must prove myself in the workplace. Yes, I get overlooked for positions. Yes, I am underpaid. Yes, I am ridiculed by women and Black men for my gender preference.

My relationship with another woman is my personal choice and is not just sexually motivated. It is about finding someone to love me and me to love them, to respect, and share a life together and grow old together; to raise a family and to pool our resources together. It's no different than the heterosexual relationship. Edwina and I found each other in high school and we are still together. We experience some of the same issues as heterosexual couples and we chose each other. We have to work on our relationship, be concerned about our finances, who is responsible for what, who will wash the car, cook and clean. We are human.

Edwina and I married in June of 2016. We had dated since high school and cohabitated since college. We had a large, elaborate and traditional wedding with a complete wedding party. The church was filled with family, friends, coworkers and we were given blessings for a successful marriage. I realize that some came out for mere curiosity to see how the event would turn out, to see which one of us would wear the gown, the tux, and who would recite the nuptials first. Many have asked me, who is the man and who is the woman?

In our LGBTQ relationships or should I say my and Edwina's relationship, it is not discussed. However, in every relationship, whether heterosexual or homosexual, there is a dominant person. In most cases, in the heterosexual relationship, we naturally think the man is the most dominant. Because of tradition, our society and biblical scripture, the man is the head of the household. Unfortunately, it does not hold true in all situations; there are women in marriages that "wear the pants" in their relationship. Does that make her the man and the husband the woman? Hmmm. We are constantly plagued with homophobia acts.

Passing the law for same sex marriage was a blessing in disguise for the LGBTQ community. We could finally be legally married with full benefits. We realize that the law granted us this opportunity to share all federal benefits but it does not change societal thoughts, beliefs and attitudes towards the LGBTQ community. We realize that making same sex marriages legal does not mean we have been accepted. We have come a long way, but we have a long way to go.

# Chapter Sixteen

The Black Woman

*"We are all gifted. That is our inheritance."*
— *Ethel Waters*

### Ava Brown

Who are we really? As Black women, are we who someone wants us to be or are we who we really are? As Black women, we are magical; we come in all skin tones, body shapes and sizes. We must define our own beauty and not measure our beauty based on the standards of other people. We are unapologetically beautiful! We are ageless and simply gorgeous. We are often met with obstacles, which we overcome and persevere. We are resilient.

We have been here since the beginning of civilization. However, many of us have been robbed of that truth. As Black women, we have been noted as having a gift of strength since slavery, when our body, mind and spirit were mutilated but that mutilation has become our strength to overcome our adversities in life. We are hurt, but we are unbreakable. We have boundless love and are capable of forgiveness. We are innately born nurturers. We take care of the children, both male and female, and they learn from us. We are their inspiration. The children's values are formed from our images.

As Black women we must get it together. We help form, both our males and females about the Black woman and Black male. If we want our girls to love self and the other Black woman, mothers must love themselves and their sisters. In order for the Black girls to grow up to love the Black man, we must show and teach them to love. This starts in the home. We are the most powerful influence for our male and female children. When we educate our children at home, we can educate the world. But first, we must know who we are as the Black woman.

We are often exhausted, misunderstood, labeled with stereotypes or viewed through distorted lenses, but we are successful and possess many talents. We all have different dreams and aspirations. Is that the reason, the White man and woman, and the Black man ridicule, stereotype, devalue and ignore the Black woman? Why does the Black woman ridicule each other? We must be who we want to be, and not be dismayed by others' thoughts and persuasions.

The Black woman must not allow anyone to place "blinders," or limitations on our capabilities intrinsically and extrinsically that keep us from accomplishing all the attainable things in life. We must keep up the fight, the fight to be understood, to fight the stereotypes that we have been labeled and break the chains that hold us back as the Black woman.

Two women are born, one a White woman and the other Black, however, the Black woman was considered second best to their White counterparts. During slavery our ancestors watched the White woman being pampered as delicately as a porcelain doll. Our Black ancestors looked from afar as our White counterparts dressed in the finest of clothing and adorned themselves among the most elite and social classes, as our ancestors slaved over hot stoves, cleaned their homes and reared their children. The pictures gave such aesthetic pleasure to the Black woman and through generations, the Black woman adopted the trends of the White woman.

Our styles, hair, body design, and language have all been put down as being unattractive. White America set the scale, so they knew we could not be high contenders in their race. Unfortunately, we became believers of this misconception and attempted to succumb and make changes to be more acceptable to White society. Big mistake. The essence of the Black culture was robbed by the White culture. Strangely, the things that the Black female struggled with to meet the demands of White society is changing.

Big lips, hips, "nappy" hair and tanned complexions are all becoming the trend among White women. Now, the White woman is emulating features of the Black woman and are going through drastic changes such as plastic surgery and tanning booths to obtain the looks that the Black woman was naturally born with.

In some cases, the Black men are hurting their nation especially when they take on the tone that White women are open to sexual fantasies and are not sexually inhibited. They aim to please. White women do not have the same issues as Black women. They seemingly open their arms to Black men and accept them for who they are, regardless. The White woman put them on a pedestal.

Some men say they don't see color — imagine that. Is the Black man trying to live up to the White man's mentality or is he suffering from a form of psychosis that he needs to repay the White man for raping the Black woman? Or does the Black man want to regain power over the White woman as the Black woman was to the White man during slavery? Is this payback?

How does the Black woman feel when she sees the Black man with a White woman, committing to a relationship and marriage? It is painful that the Black man denounces Black women and elevates White women. This is a prime example of amnesia, forgetting the fact that he has a Black mother, grandmother, sisters, and cousins. To me, it is demeaning to see a Black man with a White woman. It makes me wonder why? Why isn't he honoring the Black woman like a queen?

Doesn't he know he is contributing to the extinction of his race? If he has money, why isn't he helping a Black woman off the welfare system and poverty? What makes her different from other women? What is happening to the Black race, culture and heritage? How will either of them uphold their traditions? Is the Black woman just not good enough?

I have always told my sons to marry a Black woman. It would be a slap in the face for you to take care of a White woman, when there are Black women, Black sistas out here! Being a struggling single mother with two Black sons, knowing the hardships and prejudices they encounter as Black men, neither needed to add another racial barrier to their life. Within interracial marriages, traditions, languages and customs are lost, resulting in no true races in the near future. I knew a Black man who told his daughter if she married a White man, he would delete her from his will. He explained to her the hardships that Black men encountered from the White race and it would be an insult to him as a Black man. In some instances, the Black man who is financially secure may marry a White woman of a lower socio-economic class; that helps her to climb the social ladder, Why not the Black woman?

I believe in Black marriage and I firmly believe we need to marry within our race for our children's sake and for the sake of culture, traditions, and heritage. I often hear stories of the Black family, the struggles, the happy moments and how true love was shown. We lose out as a Black culture when our families become mixed; one or the other will not understand our history. To me this is a prime example of being unevenly yoked as two left shoes; there is no way. As I think about this, does the White man or woman in the relationship ever think about the person as being a "nigga?" That is a thought that is embedded in my thoughts.

The Black man has been made to feel below or second-class to the White man. They have been ripped of their dignity as far back as slavery. They've had to watch as their slave masters raped their wives and when they fought back they were brutally beaten or killed. The Black man lost jobs, the collapse of manufacturing jobs; the declining labor market and racial discriminations have tremendously impacted our Black men.

I believe the Black woman has the power to strengthen the Black man and help restore the meaning of Black marriages. The Black woman has the power to keep on pushing and giving the Black man the support to help him regain dignity and self-respect. I personally, do not believe that the woman has to walk so many steps behind him to do that but standing behind him, supporting him in his endeavors and supporting him while he is down can help build him up. I believe the Black woman can accomplish this and strengthen the bond between the Black man and woman without losing her own individuality.

All Black men are not alike. Some mistreat the Black woman and some of our Black men treat our Black woman like queens. When we as the

Black woman experience bad relationships often times we retaliate on the next one. We build up walls that are unbreakable and make it difficult to let the man in. We have to stop punishing the next man for the things that the previous man did to us.

As Black women, we want to be loved; the Black man wants to be respected. It's time to re-unite Black relationships and Black marriages.

Sometimes, we over play the "strong Black woman syndrome," and that drives the man away. We too want to be understood by our Black man. We want them to understand that by nature we are strong, however, we want to lean on him and to be understood.

It takes longer for some to soften up than others. We are labeled the "angry Black woman," because we don't want to hurt again and the truth be known, we desire to be with the Black man.

How do we build relationships? Don't cling on. Give the man some space. It gives each of us the opportunity to breathe and to be ourselves. We must let him know our expectations, whether is short or long term. If he cannot deal with it, he will more than likely move on. Expressing what we want will prevent pointless time. If we want a Christian man, we shouldn't expect to find him in a club. Many times, we want a man to change when we date or marry him and many times, the man don't want the Black woman to change, but we do.

Sex is important to a relationship, but sex too soon is not the foundation to a long lasting relationship. If we are in it for sex only, then we should let the person know. I heard a man say, when asking the Black woman to bake him some cookies, the Black woman's response was, "bake them yourself," but when asking the White woman, she responded, "Ok honey, what kind would you like?" Men like to see that a woman is tidy and to feed him when he's hungry. So, the adage, "the way to a man's heart is through his stomach," still holds true to most men.

We must allow the man to be the head of the household. Aren't we tired of taking on all the responsibility? If we are angry, naturally we must resolve the issue first. Once the problem is resolved, let it go. We must be supportive of our man. If he's out trying to make an honest living, then we gotta support him and let him know how much we appreciate his efforts and accomplishments. Build him up and have his back. Most of all respect him.

I say lower the sexual inhibitions in the bedroom, be spontaneous, and don't punish the man by not having sex with him. If we are angry, then naturally we won't have sex with him because first the problem needs to be resolved. Once the problem is resolved, then we have to let it go, and not keep bringing it up over and over again. Being spontaneous is a good thing and it eliminates boredom. Having sex in the same place and the same time every time for the last five years can become boring. Variety adds spice to anyone's life. We want our man to know what we want. Tell him – he is not a mind reader. Just be specific when communicating what you want.

We must keep ourselves up; if not for him, for us. When we know we have put on those extra pounds, if nothing else, take a few off, it helps us to feel good about ourselves and he will love it.

We are the matriarchs over our lives. We are strong by nature. The adversities that robbed our mind body and soul are our weapons of strength. Let's love our Blackness, we have transcended. Let's love our Black men and work on rebuilding the relationships with them and support them. Let's re-define who we are as a Black woman, re-establish our values, make the decision and live it. Let's set examples for other Black women and Black men. We will not allow anyone to tell us how we should feel or question our individuality or uniqueness anymore. We will love who we are, unconditionally.

# Reflections from the Soul

# Chapter Seventeen

"MY FIRST – I learned, that First, Does Not Always Mean Best."

*"I always wanted to be somebody. If I made it, it's half because I was game enough to take a lot of punishment along the way and half because there were a lot of people who cared enough to help me." – Althea Gibson*

## Dr. Antoinette Stroter

## Background

Despite harsh living conditions – the poverty, the gang infested neighborhood, the absent father, the part-time mother, the eight siblings (all living under the same roof) of a pregnant-with-her-ninth-child single mother, working two jobs, and the responsibility of raising eight brothers and sisters – my mother, who is the first born of 10 children, gave birth to me, her first born of two children.

My mother and grandmother were pregnant at the same time, twice, for the last two of my grandmothers 10 children. My mother dropped out of high school before the age of 18 and was the first and only of the 10 children to later get her GED. My mother was born in the drug infested neighborhoods of Chicago and later moved to East Saint Louis, Illinois where I was born. I would like to share with you the story of "MY FIRSTS."

# Birth
## First Born Child

A great place to start would be to discuss the circumstances surrounding my birth. I was born and raised in East Saint Louis, Illinois in the late 60's (the year the late Dr. Martin Luther King was murdered). My mother lived with her mother in the projects (low income government housing). I will always be my mother's **FIRST BORN** and all that comes with being a first-born. There are a few details about my life that are worth mentioning that are not atypical of first born children and, in many regards, my life was shaped by the person I fought against becoming – causing deep, emotional trauma. My absent father with whom I recently discovered (at the age of 47) has 23 children, of which I am not his first-born but fairly close. I am his second child. I was not only my mother's first born but I am also the **FIRST BORN** of my father's legacy in my family. One can probably never guess what I mean by that.

### First Born of the Booker Tribe

Well let me tell you more about my father's legacy, which landed me in another position of being the **FIRST BORN**. My mother was dating my father and got pregnant with me (her first child). She went on to have a second child with him one year later. While my mother was pregnant with her second child my father began a sexual relationship with my mother's first cousin who also became pregnant by my father. Who would have ever thought this betrayal would happen between two first cousins? It did not stop there. My mother separated my sister and me from my father and his family to shield us from all the lies, betrayal, and deceit that just kept thickening on both sides of the family. My mother's first cousin while pregnant with her second child discovered that one of her younger sisters was also pregnant by my father.

So, now, I have officially become the **FIRST BORN** of the tribe of three cousin's children. They are technically cousins, half-sisters and half-brothers. My mother's first cousin and her sister have four children each by my father and were pregnant four times, simultaneously. My father much later in life left both the first cousin and her sister. We found out that he had fathered several children outside the two members of my family to total 23 children to date.

We often joke today at family reunions; all Booker (my father's name) kids' line up for picture. I am always featured as the **FIRST BORN** of the Booker tribe/clan/era. For me this is not and never will be a joke. It is embarrassing but in today's society it would be a highly favorable episode of a popular talk show. It is a painful memory that will not stop hurting so I buried the truth or should I say rarely ever shared the story.

I grew up hating my father for having sexual relationships and children with three women from the same family at the same time. I grew up admiring my mother for removing herself from the situation where she was the victim of such deep-rooted betrayal and making something out of herself and the lives of her two children.

## My First Fight
### First Fight to Survive

Growing up in East Saint Louis you had to learn to fight. There were so many gangs and I am grateful that I was never forced to join one. I was given an option to be the queen of the gang (Park Avenue Players) because my first boyfriend was the founder and leader of that gang. I recall him hiding the gang life that he led until he shot and killed someone and went to prison. I found out then that he was the leader of this gang because he sent the gang members to protect me and my family while he was in prison. There were several threats launched against me and my family in retaliation to my boyfriend.

My **FIRST FIGHT** was within myself—trying to convince myself that I deserved to live. I had to fight the odds that I could survive in the ghetto. My first fight was for my life and to believe that I had the right to live and live life more abundantly. I believed that my destiny was to be in a gang. I also had to fight not to introduce drugs into my system because everyone else was doing it. The kids in our neighborhood were smoking marijuana (dope or joints) as we called them. No one could afford the high-end drugs. I had to set the example for my sister and two cousins. Growing up together, we could fight this fight of life and live to tell the tale to our children and grandchildren one day.

## First Physical Fight

I will never forget my **FIRST FIGHT,** which took place when I was in the third grade. I am jumping back in time to third grade for this experience. There was a young lady who was also in the third grade who I accidentally bumped into one day in the hall between classes. She went around all day telling everyone that she was going to beat me up after school. So after school there was a crowd of students waiting for me on the playground not shortly after the bell rang. I was not scared at all; my mother had taught us that physically fighting was in our blood and that we were winners.

She instilled in us to hit first and ask questions later. If anyone approaches you, fight and if they enter your personal space within swinging distance, swing first and go for parts of the body that they not be able to return the swing. We were taught to punch them in the eye or in the groin/vaginal area (any sensitive part of the body). We were also taught that if there was a rock, a stick, a brick or any object near you, pick it up and swing. The motto she would often chant was, "Sticks and stones will break your bones but words will never hurt you."

(Ironically, today, I know the opposite to be true. Whereas, bones heal over time (and usually naturally), the pain words inflict hurt far more and last a lifetime.) Once I arrived on the playground in the center of the huddle, Jeanette was awaiting me. She began swearing and cursing me calling me a Black bitch. She had been wanting to kick my ass for a long time. I just stood there and listened as the crowd egged her on. I had it coming.

She got closer and closer to me and once she was in swinging distance, though she was still chanting, I swung and hit her in the face. I was going for the eyes, but I missed. Needless to say, she came back punching, so I started kicking, missed, and she started kicking me. It was not long before teachers broke up the fight. I did not win my **FIRST FIGHT**.

By the time I got home, my mother and family had already heard about how I got my Black ass kicked and that was unacceptable. My mother took me to Jeanette's house, which was walking distance from ours. My mother knocked on the door and challenged Jeanette to come outside and fight me again.

However, no one in that house would open the door because everyone was very afraid of my mother including Jeanette's mother. Not long after that, I got into a series of fights with other students at school and I would win every fight. Many students became afraid of me just like they were afraid of my mother. I was never a bully as we call them today. I would only fight physically to defend myself when provoked.

After that **FIRST FIGHT,** I had to set the example that no one should touch or talk about me or they would "get their ass kicked." Nothing went right for me at first, including fighting. But I learned to be tough, resilient, and to stand up for myself. I actually learned that physical fighting was a way to survive in the ghetto/hood. Making others fear you worked.

I am not advocating that this is the best way as today's society, much like what the neighborhood had become by the time I was a teenager, was to fight with knives and guns to the death. I could have easily been dead by now. I know there is a God who saved me from myself, and others out in the only ghetto streets I grew up in.

### My First Kiss
### First Mouth Kiss

It would probably be ideal to talk a little about my childhood and how I grew up in the ghetto – the hood, which is where I experienced my **FIRST MOUTH KISS**. It is actually where many of my life's experiences took place, but I want to focus on my first mouth kiss, which took place when I was in the third grade and my first vaginal kiss which took place during my high school senior prom.

The third grade was such a pivotal turning point in my life. I was told by my third grade teacher, Mr. Jones, that I was smart, and a natural born leader, and not a person who had to fight with violence. He made me a patrol girl who monitored the hallways during breaks. He made me editor of the class newsletter. He would call on me first and constantly give me compliments. It wasn't long before I began to believe I was smart and a natural born leader that should use my gifts to get out of the ghetto/hood. Well, it was also in the third grade that I got my first kiss on the mouth by a man not a boy.

One of my mother's younger brothers who was over the age of 20 began showing us dirty magazines of naked people—men and women—having sexual intercourse. He actually tried to convince me to have sex with him but he never forced me to. I would always say, "No." But one, day he kissed me on the mouth for a few seconds and I got away from him. I ran and told him I was going to tell my momma. He never bothered me again and I never told anyone until now.

I had quite a few kisses on the mouth with boys of my age after that. I thought kissing was gross and I grew up a virgin. I did not have sex with a boy until prom night, which was long overdue in my school. Many of the girls were pregnant and some with the second child and they had not finished high school. I am blessed to not have fallen into that trap.

**First Vaginal Kiss**

My ex-husband, which I started dating at the end of 9th grade, was the **FIRST VAGINAL KISS**. It was prom night and I had discussed having protected sex with him. We had been dating for three years and he begged for sex, but I said no. I was waiting for marriage, which is what my mother told me to do. Well, I did not wait until marriage, but I waited until after I had graduated from high school. I went to my mother for help, which was unheard of during that time. She took me to the free clinic and started me on birth control and gave me some condoms for him to use during sexual intercourse. I was comfortable with my mother as I was proud to have made it that far without being pregnant and dropping out of high school. I think when Mr. K Jones changed my direction in life in the third grade he changed my mother's life as well. She also began to believe in me and started trying to preach and teach the importance of creating good, positive life — experiences that she never had herself growing up. She was pregnant with me as a teenager and dropped out of high school.

Prom night was another page-turner in life. I had my **FIRST VAGINAL KISS.** My ex-husband was very gentle at the time. We talked through every step before we got there. He was sweet and kind and by that time willing to wait if I was not comfortable.

He rented a room at the Red Roof Inn and after he gently placed his lips on my vagina he licked the clit a little and stopped and asked if was okay. I said, "No," and, probably a disappointment to this story, he did not go any further that night. I was too scared. It took us a couple of weeks trying to have sex before we got through our first sexual encounter. We waited two years like we promised our parents and got married and had one beautiful baby girl together.

## My First Pregnancy

My **FIRST PREGNANCY** took place with my ex-husband who was my fiancé at the time. He joined the United States Air Force and I was a student at the University of Illinois in Urbana Champaign, Illinois. We would visit each other on college breaks. Sometimes he would travel to visit me in Urbana and I would travel to visit him in England where he was serving an overseas assignment. I traveled to him in England and we took a flight to Germany to visit some friends who were stationed at a military base. I had been struggling with the pill. I had a hard time swallowing them and staying on schedule, many times skipping doses and throwing them up.

Needless to say, sexual intercourse continued despite the inconsistency in taking the birth control pills and I got pregnant three months before the wedding. We moved the wedding up and got married so that I did not walk down the aisle with a fat belly and so that I could get proper prenatal care. I dropped out of college, moved to England with him, got married, and reassigned to Little Rock Air Force base in Little Rock, Arkansas. Our baby was born.

We had a lot of challenges adjusting to one another after the birth. I was determined not to have any more children. However, I got pregnant within one year three times and all three times I had an abortion. I refused to raise more than one child on my own and I did not see us having much of a future together. But, we stayed married for 12 years, much longer than I expected. It took me 12 years to walk away from an alcoholic and a cheater. I also wanted to go back to school and I knew that would be very difficult with more than one child. I would often chant I can carry this one on my back but I refused to have anymore.

The abortions were mentally draining for him and me. We really contemplated not aborting the third pregnancy but I just could not give birth again. I actually decided not to have any more children at all and today that is still my belief. I stuck to my guns after having three blood-sucking abortions that I am too embarrassed to ever tell my child or grandchildren about.

### Conclusion

God can bless you with opportunities in life no matter where and how you grew up. I can share so many stories about my life that were page-turners. I know God intervened and sent angels to protect me. I graduated from high school 4th in my class and went to a prestigious four year institution. I obtained four college degrees – two in the sciences and two in education. The highest being a terminal doctorate of philosophy. How you start does not have to be how you end up.

# Chapter Eighteen

## Implicit Bias: The Mischaracterization
of the Black Woman

*"You may encounter many defeats, but you must not be defeated. In fact, it may be necessary to encounter the defeats, so you can know who you are, what you can rise from, how you can still come out of it." – Maya Angelou*

### Carolyn Ross

So what adjective are you going to use to describe me today? And by no means please suggest that I am just another angry Black woman with an attitude, who's highly emotional. Nor am I an ape walking around in heels. This is the exact reason why implicit bias permeates our society. We love to place these colorful labels on us Black girls. Depict us as if we are uncouth and have no home training. Irrational in thought and ready to take on anybody who we feel has disrespected us. Too often we are immediately charged with being loud and obnoxious and hard to get along with – just another mischaracterization, to say the least. At times we are even accused of "trying to be more than what we are,"(Bourgeoisie) and that we need to stay in our place. So, at the end of the day, it doesn't really matter how intelligent and gifted Black women are and that we've been accepted and have attended some of the nation's most prestigious colleges and universities.

We have to prove ourselves and our worth time and time again, having to work harder than most. Nobody has given us anything. And most of us, if asked, will reveal that we are not products of "affirmative action." It's still tragic that we have to force society to do what is right by us – equal opportunity? The government still has to intervene and force institutions to level the playing field here in the 21st century. Why?

As a Black woman, we always had to live by a double standard, having to act a certain way. Whatever happened to living by the golden rule? Treating others the same way that you would like to be treated? Is this asking too much? Can I implore that you be respectful of who we are as women and try to look past that my skin tone is darker than yours and my African American surname? Good luck. Every job application that I have ever filled out asks, "what's your race and what's your gender?"

As you continue to read my brief testament, you will come across a whole lot of "whys." It's because why me? Why did God choose me to be born into the Black race? I often ask God, "Why did the Black race have to be the race that is always discriminated against and scorned? "Why is it always a struggle for the Black man?" Society has been conditioned to measure and compare everything that we do on this earth by the color of someone's skin. Are they Black or are they White?

Why is it that Black women are often viewed as unhappy individuals walking around with this huge chip on our shoulders with a funky attitude? Don't blame us. It's not as if society didn't have its hand in helping shape and mold us into the women we are today! Black women are always expected to behave with a certain amount of passivity. I will not apologize for who I am. I am who I am. Paula Dean can say it, and America turns a deaf ear. We still buy her products, no matter the derogatory comments she made about the Black man. We have forgiven her and let bygones be bygones, as she gets richer by the minute. If a Black woman had made a racial slur or something unacceptable, we would have been met with an overreaction, deemed as being aggressive and antagonistic.

Most of us who are contributing to this book probably have experienced so many similar stereotypes and myths about this elusive Black woman. For the record, not only are we strong, intelligent and confident, we are natural born leaders in our own right. Thanks to our mothers, grandmothers and great-grand mothers. These awesome women are the ones who laid the foundation, the ones who gave us the tools and resiliency to be able to navigate in such uncertain times. This world has become very unpredictable, a not so nice world. Not that it ever has been.

Let the truth be told, I guess, I never really learned how to "play the game," the game of "going along to get along." I guess I did not take heed to grandmother's teachings, and had to learn the hard way, on the job training, "OJT" in a sense. Much that I have learned in this short life is that you can never take anything for granted. As a Black female you can easily be misunderstood and seen in a whole different perspective by others than you see yourself. We can thank societal perceptions of Black women for that. We have always been viewed through a distorted lens.

I recall my dreading taking campus climate surveys as a campus principal. I didn't want to hear any negative feedback, especially if it were about me. I always felt that I treated my faculty and staff fairly and with respect, so therefore, there is nothing bad or negative that anyone could say about how I led the school, boy was I mistaken.

Here is what was shared:
(1) Our principal is aggressive and strong-willed, but she keeps the campus safe.
(2) Our principal seemed aloof when talking with her. She is not focused on my personal needs. She looks around the room while talking.
(3) Our principal is hard-driving, no-nonsense and gets straight to the point.
(4) Our principal treats faculty and staff fairly, and has high expectations for all.

This feedback, although disconcerting and disheartening caused me to stop and take pause. It made me realize that how I viewed myself as a leader was totally the opposite of what my faculty and staff felt. It caused me to really think hard about my interactions with my teachers and my students. I could have gotten angry. My staff was disloyal to me even after everything I had done for them. I helped the campus turn around discipline and bring up test scores, but at the end of the day, I know for a fact that I could not have done it without their buy-in. In retrospect, they did have to "buy-in" to my vision at some point in time or we would not have seen the major changes and growth on the campus. Morale and climate was up, despite the feedback on the survey.

As a society, we know so little about what truly makes Black women so resilient. What exactly is our place here? How can we fit in without being judged so harshly? It's this perception of Black women, and how we are supposed to behave in order to be treated with dignity that causes everyone around us to overreact at the slightest sign of nonconformity.

I have experienced so many highs and lows in the workplace. I feel that I have often been so misunderstood as an African American female, just wanting the best for all. I pride myself in trying to be a champion for the underdog. Walking away most often feeling so unappreciated and disappointed, I am a big believer in giving people "second chances." I just wish this were the case when it comes to me. The year 2016 is one that will live in my heart forever.

This was the year that I realized that there are a lot of callous and heartless people on this earth and unfortunately in positions of power. One day you can be at your job and the next, it can all be taken away from you in a flash and without warning. I do not want to give too much of my time to an organization that allows its employees to be treated so unfairly as such. The main take away here, is that we must always remember that it all starts at the top, with the leader, good, bad or indifferent or even spineless.

I was given a "non-renewal" on my administrative contract in education for the first time in three decades as a career educator. What a blow – not only to my psyche, but to who I was as a person. For the first time in many years, I felt as if everything that I had done as an educator was in vain. I had to re-evaluate who I really was and if I had even been in the right profession all of this time. This is what someone can do to you if you allow it. Cause you to have self-doubt. You begin to question your existence. You may even start believing the stereotypes, "hard to get along with and someone who needed to be controlled by any means necessary." The reality is that no matter how hard-working, committed and loyal you may be, there was something about me that was still misunderstood and not embraced by the new leadership.

The most frightening thing through this entire ordeal is knowing that you can lose your job and work closely with the commander and chief of a district who was supposed to have been your mentor and role model. Just merciless! I was thrown under the bus and ran over for someone who was promised an extension on their contract. That just confirmed that this individual had no regard or compassion for me as human nor valued my contribution to the district and the students.

As a Black woman, I have every reason to feel disenfranchised. I have gone through every emotion that one can experience. First of all, as Black women, we constantly have to keep our guards up, making sure that we are saying and doing the right thing and being "politically" correct.

I find it hypocritical to say the least that a person can run for the highest office of the United States and have unsecured e-mails that could jeopardize our national security, while the other candidate talked about what he has done to women in the past and that is forgiven. What gives? Have we relegated ourselves as a country with just settling for this type of behavior and it is okay? I can give you a list of circumstantial accusations as to why my contract to lead a campus was non-renewed, but it pails in comparison to what our current leaders have done and are still doing.

We still live in a world of double-standards and where money "talks." If you are not a millionaire or a billionaire, then you will not come close to being considered for a cabinet position under the leadership of the new regime. Oh, that's right unless you are Omarosa. Just to try and silence us once again.

During my time being unofficially forced into retirement, I have come to dispel any myth that may be circulating out there about the strength seen in Black women. Let it be told that we are invincible and unrelenting, and that we are able to persevere and endure against great odds without being negatively affected. So untrue!

We are human and we have feelings. It is not that easy to overcome very damaging stereotypes. We get "Black-balled" no pun intended and placed in a category that makes it hard to find future employment. You can almost place us in the same category with being a felon.

As Black women, we have so much to bring to the table. Being ignored and misunderstood is what we've had to learn to endure over time. We have the ability to support and hire one another. We have the power to give second chances. In trying to accept ourselves we have to realize that we will never be fully embraced by mainstream White America. We will not let this dictate who we are as a race.

As a Black woman, I implore you to no longer be invisible and lost in society. Try to find a healthy balance that we all so desperately need and deserve in our lives. We will not be held hostage to stereotypes and myths or confused by parameters on who you think you are, or what you believe that you should or can become. We will mobilize ourselves into an impenetrable united force that will empower women all across the nation, as we become the proud and confident leaders' that God has chosen us to be.

In closing, Black women, I'm not going to totally let you off the hook either. I have come to learn that as women, we can sometimes be meaner to one another more than our White counterparts. We have historically not supported each other when we have had the opportunity. Earlier, I mentioned that we need to employ our sisters when we get in positions of leadership and please don't be a supervisor who is hard to work for.

I have encountered some of my worst job experiences in education under the supervision of Black females. I found them to be extremely oppressive, self-absorbed sisters who never had a kind thing to say about anyone or anything, unless you were one of their Sorority sisters. I could not understand how someone like them was ever allowed to be in a position of authority. Instead of viewing these women as potential mentors and someone that I wanted to learn from, I found myself never wanting to be in their presence. These women give a diary of a mad Black woman a whole new meaning. And what is so sad about that is it doesn't have to be that way. It takes a whole lot of energy to be mean and to find flaws in people, but until you are willing to look in the mirror and self-reflect about whom you are as a person, then you will never get it.

I consider myself a very confident and afro-centric sister. I wear my haircut low and no make-up. Forget the long nails and weave. I am just an all

- natural Black woman. We live in a society, where as Black women we are already made to feel as if we are not good enough, so why do we do it to one another? We have been conditioned to hate our ethnicity. As Black women, we struggle with our physical features. We have thick lips and big hips; everything about us just seems so much bigger. But guess what? Women of all races are trying to achieve this voluptuous look, Botox in the lips and implants in the hips.

Over time, I have come to embrace and love who I am. I just want other Black women to do the same. Stop being so bitter towards one another and stop wasting time on so much negative energy. We have the power to lift one another up and just be nice.

# Chapter Nineteen

I Am A Survivor, I Really Am, A Survivor

*What God intended for you goes far beyond anything you can imagine.*
— *Oprah Winfrey*

### Shawnta' Monique

When asked the question how does it feel to be a Black woman, there's one word that comes to mind and that is SURVIVOR. For me, when I think of all we endure as Black women, I feel extremely proud because it doesn't matter what comes our way, we will SURVIVE!!!

It's crazy but as a child, we see the life we want to have and think we are going to have yet it never occurs to us that it just might not happen that way. I have been married for 11 years and have been with my husband for the past 18 years. During those years, we have had our ups and downs where we would break up but regardless of the situation we would make up and pull through... at least that was the case up until 2008 when I reached my breaking point. For years I had tolerated the lies, cheating, and disrespect mainly because I truly loved this man and believed he would eventually change. I moved in with my (at that time) boyfriend straight from my parents home and had never been on my own. To do it now with two children was just not an option for me.

My husband and I moved to Texas in 2005 away from all of our family. I thought the change would be good for our relationship so one year later in 2006 we got married. I figured having only each other to depend on would strengthen our marriage but it actually did the opposite. I literally had no one but him and I believe it's why he continued to be unfaithful. He felt I wouldn't or couldn't leave. In October 2008, I had finally had enough. My self worth began to diminish because I felt I was not enough.

The emotional abuse became physical one day and that's when I knew we needed to be apart. My children were only 1 and 3 years old and I wasn't sure how we were going to make it. Although I had a job, I wasn't making enough money to support myself and my children on my own. I was not receiving any financial help but was able to get rental assistance which was a huge relief. Things were pretty tight, I didn't have that extra five dollars for a happy meal but my bills were paid, we had food on the table, clothes on our back, and I had a peace of mind so to me we were ok.......or so I thought.

One night while in the shower, I decided to do a self-breast exam, which is something I had never even thought about doing. I guess you can say it was nobody but God speaking to me that night. Well in doing, so I discovered a lump in my breast. I hate going to the doctor so I pretty much ignored it for a while but it stayed on my mind. Eventually, after talking to my mom, I decided to go see the doctor for a mammogram. My doctor sent me for a biopsy and when they were done the nurse asked if she could call me with the results or if I wanted to come into the office. Well naturally I felt I had nothing to worry about because I had a history of having cyst in my breast so I told her to go ahead and call me. In March 2009, exactly four months after separating from my husband, I received the most devastating news I was definitely not expecting to hear.

I was at work one morning when I received a call from the nurse. She identified herself then asked "sweetie are you alone" at that very moment all I could do was cry because I knew what followed. She apologized and then proceeded to tell me that my test came back positive for breast cancer. At the age of 31, I was diagnosed with stage 3 breast cancer. Just ten years prior I was told I had Lupus—now here I am being told my life may be over sooner than I expected. All I could think about was what was going to happen to my children.

When I was diagnosed with Lupus, I was told that I may never have kids, and now that God saw fit to bless me with two beautiful babies, I may

144

not be around to raise them. I was scared and felt so alone. My husband and I had just separated and I had no family close by. How could I survive this by myself? I just needed someone to hold me and say "you're going to be ok" but I never got that. After speaking to the nurse, I called my mom and best friend as well as my husband. When I couldn't reach him, I called a mutual friend who worked along side him. I left work and drove home in tears. When I made it home my friends came by to check on me but the one person I needed to be there wasn't and that was my husband.

In April 2009, I went in for surgery. My mom and friends were there to support and my husband came by briefly. My surgery was successful and the doctor removed the cancer as well as 21 lymph nodes which all tested negative so the cancer had not spread, Thank God! After surgery, my mom stayed in town for a few weeks to help me but eventually she had to return home. In June, I began chemotherapy treatments. That was definitely a hard process to go through alone. I did have some great friends who were very supportive and I will always be grateful for them but again, the person I needed was not there.

Having to drive myself to every doctor appointment and every chemo treatment alone was a very painful experience both emotionally and physically. During my treatments, I would sit and watch as the other patients had their family and/or spouse by their side, and I would just cry because I sat alone. The nurse would come by and ask if I was okay and all I could say was "I'll be fine." After my treatments, I would drive myself home feeling extremely weak and sick to my stomach and still have to be there to take care of my one year old and three year old. My husband still had a lot of bitterness towards me because I left so he would pick the kids up from daycare and drop them off to me not really caring if I could handle them or not. To him, it was his way of punishing me. At times I would be in so much pain that my friend would come over and help me with the kids or take them over to her house so I could rest. It was painful to know I couldn't depend on my husband, regardless of what we were going through, I was still his wife.

Shortly after starting chemo my hair began to shed. I remember the first day it happened like it was yesterday. I had just come home from a treatment. My kids were still at daycare so I was alone. I sat at the table in my kitchen looking out the bay window just reflecting over everything. I started running my fingers through my hair and as I did, my hands were full of hair. I just began to cry, pull and cry was all I could do. I had always had long hair and for a Black woman to lose her hair is traumatic, at least it was for me. As the days passed, my hair shed more and more so I realized it was time to just shave it off, and so I did.

Eventually, I began to feel really depressed with all of the emotional as well as physical changes that I was experiencing. After having a double mastectomy and going through breast reconstruction my body just wasn't the same. I had no feeling in my breast and to me they just didn't look normal. Although the cancer was only in the right side I decided to have both breast removed because the chances of the cancer returning in the other side were extremely high and I couldn't go through this all over again.

My body and overall appearance had changed and I couldn't take it. I felt as though my womanhood had been taken away and there was nothing I could do about it.

Once I had completed chemo, my doctor started me on the "after chemo pill" but after a few months she discovered it wasn't working effectively so she had to start another medication that required my ovaries to be shut down in order for it to be effective. In January 2010, I had to have a hysterectomy, which sent my depression through the roof. I felt everything that made me a woman was gone and I was useless.

At 31 years old I was having menopausal symptoms due to the hysterectomy, I couldn't have any more children, my hair was gone, and my body was disfigured, it was all just too much to deal with. I started to feel embarrassed and ashamed of my body. Through all of this I knew I had to pull myself together because I didn't want my children to see me in this state of mind.

By the end of 2011, my husband and I had reconciled and began to rebuild our family. The time apart helped us to be better for each other. I still struggle with my own insecurities about my body. I hide when I get undressed in front of my husband or I always make sure my top is covered because I just don't feel appealing.

My husband has truly been amazing this time around. He is always telling me that I am beautiful and I love him for that. But for me, things will never be the same because I feel I've lost a lot of who I am. Through it all, I wake up each morning and I thank God for the life I was given because it has taught me that I was not built to break. I was made to survive anything and everything life brings my way. I am a Black woman who can and will SURVIVE!

# Chapter Twenty

Ain't No Black Like Mine

*We can say,"Peace on Earth." We can sing about it, preach about it or pray about it,*
*but if we have not internalized the mythology to make it happen inside us,*
*then it will not be. — Betty Shabazz*

## Takyra Stephens-Chambers

I have always been the tallest (girl), which means I've got to stand at the back
when it was time to take class pictures. I have always been the darkest
African American girl in the class, which caused me to stand out even more.
On top of all that, from about the age of nine until twelve, my mother saw it
best for me to sport the juiciest, curliest jheri curl ever. Let's do some very
basic math—amazon plus dark-skin and factor in jheri curl (while other girls
had long, pressed hair or even relaxers). That equals ME being bullied—
verbally that is. Takyra Menae Stephens is the name I was given. Most of
my life, I was referred to as Menae—pronounced "Muh-Nae"; to this day my
mother is quick to correct others that pronounce it the way she (and family)
does saying, "It's 'Meee-Nae'!" Hilarious!

I am a native of Fort Worth, Texas—born and raised. I entered this
world on Tuesday, July 1, 1980 at 1:14am. Different indeed—who
memorizes information as such from their birth certificate? Me, that's for
sure. Different is something I have always noticed about myself yet
embracing it required another level of awareness. Raised by a mother who

ruled with an iron fist and with a brother, Kyron, as the primary father-figure who was also my friend. My father was my peace as a girl; just being around him was invigorating, for he was Superman—made no mistakes in my eyes, and Mom was the kryptonite. You can infer that arguing was our formal communication method. In retrospect, who was I to disrespect this woman? I was different—rebelliously different.

Religion was indeed important in my house; my mother (and family) was (and still are) devout Christians. We were in church almost every time the doors of the church were open—Sunday school, 11:00 service, 3:30 service—on Sundays; choir rehearsal on Thursday; and youth usher board meetings. I may have had the summers off from school but not church because there was vacation bible school. Even in the car, there was church via Heaven 97 KHVN—the Dallas/Fort Worth gospel station. Every now and then, we listened to Smooth Jazz 107.5.

I mocked what I saw throughout my 20s because that was all I knew —pray, have faith, and heaven would be mine. I believed that in order to be successful in life, I too, needed to be at church every time the doors opened, and that in order to see monetary success, I needed to pay tithes—off my gross and not the net. Fast forward into grown woman status, I have a genuinely profound understanding of life and spirituality; as a result, I NOW say, "Thank you Most High for shedding new LIGHT on everything and whatever will be WILL BE!"

When I was nine, my father, THE Leon J. Stephens Jr., moved to Abilene, Texas (circa 1989), and a large part of me left with him; I cried endlessly because I felt like the portion of normalcy that I possessed hit I-20 West. The end result left me in search of normalcy through the "love" and attention of males. Be clear, Mama did not raise a fool, so I didn't "DO" anything in my search, but the crushes were real and painfully disappointing every time.

In the summer of 1991, I was given a "two summer and one academic school year" chance to leave Fort Worth and live with Dad. Living with him was perfect in my eyes; it was music. Even though I had the same religious lifestyle with Dad (dad was the church's minister of music and I was in the youth choir—go figure huh), life overall was different. Life was exposure. LJ, as he is called, was (and still is) a good guy who lives by Christian principles, yet he enjoyed life a lot more. Because Dad was who he was, exposure to friends of various ethnicities and cultural backgrounds, real life vacations, and my absolute favorite—various genres of music was our life.

In retrospect, my love of music comes from living with Dad. From Luther Vandross's "Creep" to Anita Baker's "Fairytale," music has been a haven for me. I had the opportunity to be the typical girly tom-boy child including sleepovers, camp at the Boys & Girls Club and city recreation centers, Saturday mall adventures, taking care of my four-legged big brother, cutting the ginormous (or what seemed to be) front yard with Dad. It was the watching of sports with Dad that contributed to my love of basketball and football. These enriching experiences shaped my unique, quirky approach in working with the diverse population of students that I have encountered. The approach has contributed to my success as an educator.

The "two summer and one academic school year" came to a close at the conclusion of summer 1992. While consenting to the conditions of the deal, once it ended, I reneged; I could not fathom the idea of leaving home. However, I had to; Mom was hell bent on me moving back to Fort Worth. Looking back, Mom had her reasons for wanting me back with her; for time's sake, I'll just say, she missed her baby girl.

The effects of the move sparked a side of me that haunted me until I was old enough to recognize it. I became rebelliously defiant, and Mom's reaction became habitual and routine; although deserving of the consequences—physical and grounding, I became numb to them. Mom and I argued religiously, to no avail. I felt as if she did not know more than me. It wasn't until I was either 16 or 17 that I learned to just SHUT UP because I never won the argument. It took my sister-in-law, Malissi, to tell me to shut up—after hearing me go back and forth with Mom for years. Once I tried and sealed my lips, things got easier plus my senior year was around the corner.

Graduating from high school was MAGNIFICENT for me! The date was May 22, 1998 when I walked across the stage at Wilkerson-Greines.

All of the hard work I invested had a major return when I heard the mispronunciation of my name summoning me to receive my Advanced Honors diploma. Four years of intense focus earned me a $12,000 scholarship to Jarvis Christian College, a small HBCU located in the piney woods of East Texas. This scholarship covered roughly 85% of my tuition, room, and board. What wasn't covered by this scholarship was paid by two other local scholarships (based on grades) and grants. The aforementioned information is always shared with students to emphasize that really grades are important, especially if their parents (or grandparents) are not building college funds for them. Mine did not—for whatever reason.

College was THE ultimate life lesson for me. I was responsible for sure—grades were acceptable—Dean's List many semesters; I actually stayed at 3.0 or greater. There were other life lessons that have remained the most vivid. If you will recall, Dad's absence left me in search of "love"—a search for "love" because what I needed was no longer around. With this being said, I experienced "puppy love" for the first time as a freshman in college. Again I experienced "puppy love" not the dude I loved—go figure.

After about two years of mourning that "love" lost, I moved forward only to experience "real love"; once again I received the short end of the deal. What was so real about the "real love" was that I allowed myself to remain in limbo for almost eight years. Throughout this encounter, I just felt like love didn't love me. I wanted to give up, but LOVE wouldn't let me. In hindsight, I realize I had to go through all of this—most of which I put myself through—led me to examine myself thoroughly. What I discovered was that I was giving 100% of myself, and unfortunately, there was no reciprocity. This was the pure unadulterated truth.

Dad has always been the parent that I could turn to for anything, so naturally, I wanted his spill on why love did not love me. So, at our father-daughter date (circa 2007), Dad shared, "It is what it is—no more, no less." LJ explained that I was a good girl, and most guys simply don't want to mess up the good ones, and that just is what it is. You mean to tell me that in my search from 12 years of age until 27, this was all I needed to understand?! Yes indeed.

With this new perspective, I decided to seek a friendship first before imagining myself as "Mrs." Anybody. Of course it would be another two years before I put this plan into action. Once I decided to focus more on the inner me in order to create and display a better me and my short and long-term goals, life became more purposeful. The purposefulness manifested in a beautiful union—a joining of two like-minded souls into one fully functioning locomotive. Now I can definitely say, "What God has brought together—no man is able to put asunder! Ashe'! Ashe'!"

"Takyra, you should take some education courses and consider teaching!" said Mrs. Williams, my collegiate mentor and confidant. "Ohhhhh, but noooo; kids are baaaaddd," I replied. How did I go from "Ohhhh, but noooo…" to accepting an offer to teach 7th ELAR and coach ladies' volleyball and basketball? Mind you, I was not an education major, and had no plans on entering a classroom, except for maybe sitting in on my niece and nephew's classes.

In the beginning it was called *I need to get outta Mama's house by any means necessary*! But, as the year progressed, it became less about *by any means necessary* and a check and more about encouraging the less encouraged; instilling academic and behavioral discipline and responsibility; creating a mentally, physically, and academically safe environment for all. It all began in the fall of 2002; in addition, I was the assistant girls' volleyball coach and head girls' basketball coach. After a very productive first year as an educator, I did not plan on a second year, let alone fourteen more. I was grateful for the experience, but I just knew that I would proceed with MY plans, which were to move to Houston and enroll at Texas Southern University to earn a Master's degree in Speech Communications.

MY plan included an internship that would certainly lead me down the path to becoming a radio personality. But, life sometimes has its way of putting you in uncomfortable refining situations in order to set you on a path to fulfill your purpose, which isn't always to benefit you. Now that's uncanny, yet surreal. When moving to Houston to proceed with MY plans simply did not happen, I found myself working at a few different places to find out where I fit since Houston wasn't in life's plan to include Target, Dallas

County Juvenile Department—Youth Village, Dollar General, and even substitute teaching. Substituting the ONE time I did presented a life-changing moment.

A student that I did not have before said, "I just knew you were going to be my seventh grade teacher; when I didn't see your name on my schedule, I was disappointed!" Thinking to myself, "That's so sweet, but why would she want to be in MY classroom?" In other words, I did not see who she saw as an educator. But, again, life sometimes has its way of putting you in uncomfortably refining situations in order to set you on a path to fulfill your purpose. As the old Spiritual goes, "…we'll understand it betta by and by!" *By and by* occurred years after I made the decision to continue in education. The young girl will never know how her desire to be in my class encouraged me.

I discovered that the reward was in student achievement and appreciation, for their *achievement reflects their understanding* of what has been taught, and their *appreciation is encouragement* to move forward. This reassures me that the right things have been done to ensure students are given the optimal opportunity to obtain a free education.

In my introduction to students, every year, I share that I look forward to learning from them just as much if not more than they learn from me because I am dedicated to being a lifelong learner. This usually establishes that they, too, are experts in areas that educators are not—makes them feel special. Now, in my fourteenth year in education, I believe that each year has been a part of my purpose. Dwelling in my purpose has not been easy; sure there have been better years than others, but again, *by and by*, I've put together a *toolbox* of resources that continuously compel me to self-reflect and improve. My (appropriate) transparency has afforded me the opportunity to build solid, root-connected rapports with students. My *madness* is not initially welcomed, but *by and by* students accept and later on appreciate the expectations that I set for them and consistently enforce.

Prominent Black, female role models in my life include former teachers, Mrs. Griggs (kindergarten), Mrs. King (4th grade), Mrs. Pinkston (8th grade English)—these teachers, through their words and actions gave me confirmation that I was important. Seeing them in their roles, in retrospect, became a part of my teacher DNA. I must also take my hat off to my mother and one of her sisters, my Aunt Willette—both set expectations—spoken and unspoken because they KNEW that things came to me easily early on, so mediocrity was never accepted.

I am indebted to Mrs. Joan L. Williams, my college mentor, because clearly she saw teacher engrained in me. Hearing her state that I should take a few education courses and *at least* get my teacher certification, my denial of her suggestion, and now having a successful career *in education* reaffirms that *by and by* we'll understand how our plans take backseats to our soulful purpose. All of the aforementioned Black women (and others) have been role models in my existence.

In today's educational system, we are expected to do what is *in the best interest of the student*; however, very little is actually done/implemented that is in our students' best interests. Unfortunately, many students bear the weight of adult issues due to being put in an adult's shoes. There aren't many parents that invest academic/behavioral expectations into their children, so once these children display less than acceptable, well less than tolerated behavior, they are referred to counselors for *testing*. And, there you have it… another minority placed under an umbrella that only handicaps them academically. With that being said, I wish teachers like those I came through were welcomed in today's society. In addition to this, I truly wish parents were more involved with their children from the beginning, for they are their child(ren)'s first educator.

As a Black woman, I feel royal, a queen, and humbled. I believe that all women, especially Black women, should exude royalty because we are the backbone of society. James Brown sang it best, "This is a man's world but it wouldn't be nothing, nothing without a woman or a girl!" If every woman respected each other's QueenDOMness, we would conquer more. All too many times, Black women receive intimation from others. The effect is ongoing intimidation and power proving—for those in positions of power. When there is a power trip, the unknowingly intimidating sister is left feeling *less than*.

I tell students that no one makes it in this world without asking for and receiving help – so, getting help (or clarity) is essential to success. With that being said, it is important for Black women to support one another. First and foremost, we honestly need no alleviate the stereotypes—Black women are *loud, have attitudes,* and *are lazy, welfare-recipients.* The sooner we realize that these systems are in place to *help OUR* families, are actually set up to destroy them. Secondly, we have younger generations looking to us for the *way* to go, so ideally we want to show them unity in the face of conflict.

I share with students yearly that I have never been involved in a physical altercation; they are usually in awe because in their encounters, for the most, this is an anomaly. I witnessed a young lady in the school restroom screaming at the top of her lungs in front of the mirror. I figured something was wrong when I initially heard the screams. Once I investigated and simply saw this was a choice she was making, I was immediately disappointed. She was instructed to get back to class and that her behavior was unacceptable.

Of course, she caught an attitude, but once I told her that the attitude would not be tolerated because her actions were inappropriate, she got it together and made her way back to class. Now, students don't just do things like that unless they have seen it done. So, we have got to be more aware of what we do and say because they are watching us.

Life, by no means, has been silver-spoonish; however, by any means necessary I remain optimistic—it is just embedded in my melanin-rich DNA to persevere. My purpose is ever-manifesting because I tend to find purpose in all that I encounter—why not right! Being raised in Christian homes, I learned to rely on a higher power. But, in my adult hood, I have grown to realize that having a relationship with the Most High is spiritual with no weekly or monetary routines to abide by. Once I was able to recognize I was living a routine-centered versus relationship-centered lifestyle with God, it was easy to readjust. Since then, life has become easier.

I want to encourage anyone that reads this to keep an open mind in all encounters, for you never know what you can gain from the experience. In addition, understand that whatever is FOR YOU will be FOR YOU, and it will manifest in YOUR FAVOR, and you, too, will understand the Creator's plan *by and by.* —*Ashe'*

# Reflections from the Soul

# Chapter Twenty-One

## Benita's Truth

*"All great achievements require time." – Maya Angelou*

### Benita Thomas

How does it feel to be an African American woman? I am so much more! Real or imagined, true or false, right or wrong...I am more. I'm not quite sure how to answer this question. Where do I start? How much do I tell? How much do I hide? These are some of the many questions I asked myself when I was asked to participate in this project. The first thing I did was prayed and asked God if this was of Him. I needed to know if bearing my heart and soul and exposing my truth was what He wanted.

I knew this would mean sharing some things that I am ashamed of as well as potentially bringing shame to others. I am aware I need to be still in order to hear clearly what God wants me to write, as all the glory is His. I am not a writer in any way but through God all things are possible. This is written from my heart, which is the only way I will participate in this. I will lean on God and express myself and in doing so I have faith that nothing but good will come from this.

In order to get to the heart of my story I need to dig deep and peel back all of my layers of protection. This may sound easy but at 50 years old I have been in hiding for a long time. I had to examine many of my "cover stories", you know what I mean...the things I told myself and others in order to be okay. These cover stories helped me "comfortably" hide my pain of my three failed marriages/three baby daddies and childhood wounds. The thing about hiding is that you can't hide forever and the pain is not gone it's just buried. Pain in hiding is like a sinkhole, it looks normal until the surface caves. When you peer inside the hole all you see is a deep open pit of nothingness.

To be able to explain who I am as an African American woman I must share my story…not everything, but the parts that have challenged me. This has helped mold me into who I am as a woman…an African American woman. My prayer is that my story will reach people of all races, cultures, religions and backgrounds. But mostly I pray that someone out there will know that through the love of God and His grace and mercy it will be okay.

*Benita's truth…my upbringing*

I was born in Newark, NJ in the winter of 1967. I was the second girl child born to Nathaniel and Berta Phipps. The month after I was born, my parents purchased a beautiful house in Orange, NJ. My sister, mother, father and I resided in that house until we moved to upstate New York in 1979.

My father was born to West Indian immigrants from the small island of St. Kitts/Nevis. He grew up economically challenged as would be expected for an uneducated, Black immigrant coming from a poor country and trying to care for 9 children. The lack of finances does not mean, lack of love, lack of discipline or lack of structure! My father grew up in a very close-knit family where the love was felt and shared. My father is a twin and the very last child born to Frances O'Loughlin and John Phipps. My grandparents insisted that their children study hard, get a good job, and "make something of their selves" and that they did! Not only were they all hard workers, my father and his twin were exceptional musicians.

My mother is the oldest of six siblings and was born in the little town of Reidsville, N.C. Mom was the only one of the six children with a different father. Since she was the oldest and female she was responsible for helping to cook clean, and care for her younger siblings while her parents worked at the tobacco factory. My mother was a strikingly beautiful young woman with determination to move out of the little town she grew up in with aspirations of being a nurse as encouraged by her grandfather.

My mother was raised by her grandparents because her mother married a military man and traveled with her husband. This was no life for a little girl so she resided in the "country" with her grandma Birdie and grandfather Eugene. Though she was adored by her grandparents, she longed to be with her mom. Once her mother divorced her military husband she remarried a wonderful man named James and they had five children of their own. My mother's biological father lived on the same street with her but he never acknowledged her existence.

She would walk past his house every day to go to school, without ever so much as a wave from the man that she knew participated in creating her. Though she refuses to admit it, I am sure this has had an impact on her.

My parents met when my mother was 17 and my father was 27. My mom told my father that she was older than she actually was. They dated for many years and were married in June of 1964. They will celebrate their 53rd wedding anniversary this year.

My older sister is learning disabled which runs heavily on my father's side of the family. My parents were very dedicated to providing support for her in making sure that she was in a progressive school and was being pushed to excel. This may not seem like a big deal but in the late 60's and early 70's, children like my sister were not expected to do much and in some cases were institutionalized. To my parents credit, my sister has been able to do much more than anyone expected and has lived a very good life. Since my sister required so much attention early in life I missed out on some of the nurturing that I craved as a small child.

I developed the self-soothing habit of "rocking", my family called it "bumping". I did this as a child until I became self-conscious of it because people began to talk about me. At that point I went from public "rocking" to hiding in my room and I would rock for hours. This went on until I was in my early 30's. It wasn't until I saw a documentary about a mental institution and saw people "rocking" that I realized that I needed to heal that childhood trauma.

*Benita's truth…God humbles me*

On August 7, 2015 my life as I knew it was over. Betrayal, lies, and deceit from the very person I thought would always love me was staring me in my face. It was like I had fallen asleep and was living a bad dream. The funny thing about the Holy Spirit is that if you listen He will guide you. The bad thing for me was that I had not yet started my Christian walk. I was still relying on my own strength and giving myself the credit for the good things in my life. I had a recurring nightmare for years about the very thing that was happening to me in my marriage.

If only I had paid attention to my dreams and followed that nagging feeling in my gut. One day my friend and business developer invited me to attend church with her. What did I have to lose? I had dropped 40lbs in 6 weeks, I was losing my hair, I was in emotional turmoil, and last but not least I had lost my will to live. The place that I called home had become a museum of bad memories, and a constant reminder of how I had once again failed. When God whispers listen because when He yells it's not pretty. God was yelling for me to come back to Him and I was finally ready to turn my life back over to Him. It's not about how many times you fail, but how you dust yourself off and choose to carry on.

Now I know that God has a greater plan for my life but the person I was married to was holding me back from that plan. I was more interested in serving my husband than I was serving the Lord. Just for the record that is never a good choice. I decided to look at this as a positive thing instead of a negative thing. My ex was free to pursue his new girlfriend and I was free to pursue my new relationship with Christ. As I said before, I had three failed marriages, which up until today was a source of shame and embarrassment for me.

Today I am making the choice to declare that is my past and I will no longer be held hostage to shame and fear regarding this matter. I am a better person for having been through my experiences and I can hear God more clearly as it relates to His calling and His plans for me. He has also been able to put a mirror in front of me and show me some of my areas that need work as well as an opportunity to forgive myself.

Sometimes in life we make firm decisions about other people, but once we have an experience it sheds light on the situation. This allows us to see things differently and heal areas of our life. I want to end this section by forgiving myself for the part I played in the demise of my marriages and the pain and suffering it caused my three sons. I also want to ask for forgiveness from my three ex-husbands for any pain that I may have caused them. Lastly, I am forgiving W.M., J.T, and G.I for the pain and anguish that I suffered at your hands. I am wishing all of you love and light blessings, good health and prosperity. Thank you to each of you for my beautiful gifts…Nate, Sal, and Joshua.

*Benita's truth….from weakling to the strongest woman I know…my letter to my mother*

Dearest Berta Mae, you are my strength, you are my guide, you are my joy, you are my best friend but first and foremost you are my mother. You love immensely, you critique harshly, you stand firmly, and you nurture like an angel sent from above. We were at odds for a large part of my life and at certain points I questioned if you loved me, heck I questioned if I loved you.

However, no matter what…I always knew that as long as you were alive I have a home to return to. You single handedly held me down during my darkest moments over the better part of a year. You allowed me to cry, be angry, laugh and sometimes just be silent. You and dad would stay on the phone with me for hours and I know that you both spent many sleepless nights.

Without you and dad I would not have made it. God knew this day would come and he prepared you to say and do all the right things. I always thought that I was the strong one but God took this opportunity to show me that it was you that carried the strength. One day I asked you, "mom, how did you stay with dad during his years of infidelity?

Did you know that when you all would fight I would sleep by the adjoining room so I could protect you?" Your reply to me was, "I am sorry you felt you had to do that, I know you must have been scared. I stayed with your father because I knew that I could not provide a good enough life for you. I wanted you and your sister to have the opportunity to have all the best things in life. Natalie is disabled and moving back to North Carolina would have been very bad for her and not the best for you either. I figured sacrificing my happiness was more important than sacrificing you and your sister's opportunity to thrive in life."

My next question was, "Well how long did you have to sacrifice your happiness mom?" Your reply was, "I don't know for sure, but it was years." I began to cry. It reminded me of the "Footprints in the Sand" poem when the man was walking in the sand and he asks God why during his darkest moments God left him? God answered, "It was then that I carried you". All along I thought I was sleeping by the door to protect you but in essence it was you that was protecting me.

God used my time of suffering to show me my mother's strength. I never felt closer to my mother than I did after that call. Thank you mom for your love and sacrifice. Had I known then what I know now I would have been a better daughter. I would have loved you harder and appreciated your presence. I thank God for showing me this before I was saying this at your funeral...

I want to end this part by acknowledging my three mother-in-laws: Big Lou, Mama Bess, and Miss Nana – three queens with walks of their own! You are all very different but you all have a strength that I admire. Two have gone on to be with the Lord, you are gone but never forgotten. Thank you all for pouring in to my life...

*Benita's truth...it ain't over 'til it's over.*

January 17, 2016 was the day that I decided that I could not go on. My Uncle had just turned 60 and his wife threw him a surprise birthday party and the entire family was in town for his celebration. It was a formal event so I got dressed to the nines. I had to force myself to go because of the pain and sadness I was feeling due to my marital separation and pending divorce. It just so happened this would have been our 13th wedding anniversary as well.

I remember calling my little sister and telling her I can't go on. I was sitting in my car with it running trying to talk myself out of going inside my house and doing something. I didn't have any specific plan but I knew I was capable of doing something to myself. I remember looking up and seeing my youngest son looking at me in the car from his bedroom window.

My sister knew something wasn't right so she stayed on the phone with me and announced to my uncle and my aunts that they needed to get to my house immediately. I also called my girlfriend and added her to the call and they all began to pray for me as they piled into my uncles car to get to my house. So if you don't have a prayer warrior team, you need to get one! My prayer posse: Shug, Silver fox, TT, LMJ, Angel. They showed up at my house with holy water, holy oil, and the bible. Those ladies casted out demons, broke strongholds, and in the end sealed all the entry points to my home.

I can honestly say I was delivered that day and was on the road to true healing. No weapon formed against me shall prosper…from that day until this one every morning at 6am this message pops up on my phone…I would like to send a special thank you to my African American sister Queen prayer warriors who came out that day and saved my life. Thank you God for not being done with me…

*Benita's truth…I am an African American woman, but I am so much more…Or am I?*

First and foremost I am a child of the most high and without Him I would be nothing. African American women come in all shapes and sizes, colors and religions, experiences, strengths and weaknesses. There is an ancestral swagger that we as African American women possess.

The African American women that we see today are the ancestors of those slaves brought over to this country via slave ships… we are the great great grandchildren of those middle passage survivors. We are strong, we are wise, we are proud, we are capable. Mostly we are sisters in a way that is unspoken, a connection that is unseen and a history that is unmatched. Why don't we as sisters support each other more? Why do we go on reality television and demean and disrespect each other? Why don't we live up to our potential? Why have we forgotten that we are a proud people with a divine purpose and an opportunity to be great? Why my sisters, why? *Benita's truth…Free at Last*

So now you ask, how does it feel to be an African American woman? But I am so much more! Real or imagined, true or false, right or wrong...I am more. I'd like to end this chapter with a verse from the Nina Simone song, "I wish I knew How It Would Feel to be Free". I wish I could give all I'm longin' to give. I wish I could live like I'm longin' to live. I wish I could do all the things that I can do and though I'm way overdue I'd be starting anew." Thank you God for this opportunity to start anew and granting me my freedom...

Love and Light,
*Benita*

# Chapter Twenty-Two

## Say It *Loud…*

*"We have chapters of our lives that we fearfully keep to ourselves.*
*We refuse to believe that those are the chapters that depict us as human and admirable."*
— *Taryn Andre*

### Heather R. Sanders

Loud. A bit odd, relatively witty, moderately intelligent but definitely loud. And when you're black and female, loud is not exactly a compliment – you're either angry, bitter or maybe even both. Your facial expressions, mannerisms, body language, attitude, and tone, are always *doing the most.*

I realize, however, that my particular brand of *sass* is relatively, socially acceptable, entertaining even, so long as it never calls attention to dysfunction. And when you have a natural inclination to question or challenge age-old rituals, one of the worst places you can find yourself is a particular type of traditional black church. Being a critical, independent thinker is typically considered negative and, in many instances, blasphemous.

Being confident, authentic, unapologetic was terribly destructive and, quite frankly, offensive. We were discouraged from referencing our abilities or accomplishments and instead, prefaced any accomplishment or "blessing" as something undeserved or extraordinary in light of our unworthiness. Our salvation and our feelings about salvation were governed by church leadership. Toxic church leadership – usually black, male, undereducated, victims of abuse, turned Jesus bullies.

To be somewhat rational and black and female and *saved*? Well. The struggle was real.

Every aspect of our lives was ruled and decided by the church's leadership. The more ridiculous our lives, the more we were serving God's purpose. We were humiliated publicly and mercilessly – emotionally and spiritually exploited. We were taught that our steadfast obedience glorified God and questions or objections were blatant acts of defiance. "Loud-mouthed women" were problematic, argumentative, unfit for marriage...a marriage that was likely *arranged* because natural attraction and genuine love for another was inappropriate and frowned upon in lieu of the church leader declaring you compatible.

Church leadership concerned itself with the most ridiculous of personal matters – from approving social gatherings such as a child's birthday party, or a high school graduation celebration dinner to choosing a woman's wedding gown. Disengagement from 'the world' – proms, homecoming games, bowling, movie theaters, avoiding jewelry, makeup, and pants – was all necessary. It was visible, tangible proof that we loved God but more importantly, loved and respected the church leader and honored his word above all.

Appearances were everything. Others needed to perceive perfection (at least from your outward appearance). And our humanity was no excuse for imperfection or transparency. With the belief that each act either catapulted you into heaven or plummeted you directly into hell's torment, you and your soul were constantly in the balance, unaware of where you stood with God or the church. This constant loneliness left us feeling inadequate to define our own belief system and establish our own convictions.

Our pastor insisted we (even children and young adults) share details of our sexual experiences with him, without the consent or support of parents or guardians. But even they believed God's forgiveness depended on our willingness to share those details. Somehow, we believed he held God's mercy in the palm of the same hand that likely stroked his privates as we told our most intimate stories. He was benefitting from our vulnerability and desire to feel connected to God.

And our wallets had to be equally as open. Money could buy status and exemption from rules those less fortunate found themselves bound by. Financially supporting the church's agenda became far more important than financing a home, a child's education, or an occasional vacation. Personal or family activities that redirected potential funds for the church's misuse were often the subject of leadership gossip. Monetary contribution records were often posted in common areas for all to see and those whose gift was deemed unacceptable were called by name and openly mocked. If, in any instance you were less than fully supportive, rest assured you would hear about it.

Education was the devil's clever way of luring young adults away from God because participation in the local church was the highest priority. Education encouraged independent thinking and independence was evil. When exposed with choice, they knew we were ill-prepared to make reasonable decisions and discouraged the tedious process of thinking and deciding all together. Those who dared to relocate for college education were ungodly and clearly loved themselves more than they loved God.

There were occasional breaks...at least for me. I would be personally asked to organize important church events or activities that would, in turn, filter some of that importance into my psyche. Tragically, however, certain others were treated poorly much more often, simply because of their appearance, where they lived, who their family was or wasn't, or because their desperation was far too apparent.

During one particular youth service, when I was about seventeen, I remember being asked to sit in the pulpit with three other young people. At some point, the pastor asked me to join him at the podium. I walked slowly to him. I scrambled to find something wrong (with me), but I couldn't. I was perfect! My hair was subtle. My skirt nearly scraped the ground and my sweater was loose and long-sleeved. Socks and tennis shoes completed my overly modest ensemble.

With an bare face and traditional apostolic get-up, I was convinced he was finally bringing me forward to acknowledge my academic excellence, my leadership, my faithfulness to church, or my dedication to my family responsibilities. As I drew closer to him, I gave him an anxious grin. I had been waiting for this moment. All had been worth it for this moment.

Unusually, I could not even guess what was about to happen. But I allowed myself to be excited for, well…me. Detecting his mannerisms was an art I had mastered, but unfortunately, I was ill-prepared. In his disapproving growl, he began wagging his judgmental finger. He angrily drew attention to the "H-I-L-F-I-G-E-R" patched across my oversized athletic sweater. He convinced the congregation that I had worn the sweater to draw attention to my breasts. He decided the designer's patchwork was a demonic scheme to lure otherwise innocent men to be tempted sexually. (Never mind it was a male's sweater.)

As I was excused to return to my seat, I became physically weak. I could barely convince my body to move. Although this behavior from him was not unusual, it was unexpected. I watched my hands shake, unable to control them or the tears that fell immediately from my face. In that moment I wondered, *"Who cares about being visible, used, acknowledged when you're in prison?"* And I was in prison.

This train-of-thought led me to recall portions of my former pastor's history. He often incorporated childhood stories into his sermons. I remember him recalling financial and physical hardships his parents faced while raising fifteen children. He talked about how his mischievous brother hid from his father as he anticipated a beating. While his brother hid under the bed, his father took a leather strap and whirled it wildly under the bed striking his young son wherever the strap landed. He told that story with a sense of pride and a comedic overtone, as if his father were a disciplinarian hero. Physical abuse was the norm in his home and he had not only convinced himself that he and his siblings were better for it, but that we were better Christians for enduring his abuse.

His father and mother died during his early adolescent years and he was sent to live with an uncle who pastored a church in Iowa. He believed this launched his ministry and began his training as an apostolic preacher. He would watch his uncle publicly humiliate his own congregants, explaining their transgressions to crowds of (likely frightened) parishioners. He would often disrupt the worship service in fits of outrage to intentionally bring about shame and embarrassment.

These stories were told in laughter and we were encouraged to acknowledge him and similar ministers as forerunners and substantial figures in the apostolic movement. And as is typical, wounded children usually and understandably become *wounding* parents.

Religious bullying is a pervasive and often celebrated practice and, unfortunately, black women (as supporters of sorely unhealthy churches) are active participants in their own abuse.

Historically, black folks become comfortable surviving, rather than thriving. And although the inception of the black church was inspired by white supremacists and continues to be led by white supremacist ideologies, those who find themselves in unhealthy religious organizations are unable to muster enough courage to lean into discomfort and challenge traditional church practices. These good-hearted, well-intentioned church goers passively participate by ignoring these common sensical indicators of religious abuse at the hands of church leadership:

1. COMMUNISM. The church's culture is based on a single leadership character. His or her moods, feelings and behaviors dictate the overall climate. All decisions and ideas must pass through this figure. Ideas are good or bad based on this character's reaction or lack thereof.

2. THE BIPOLAR. The leader is unkind, moody, cruel and has unreasonable expectations. For example, he or she has extremely varying responses or reactions to similar situations depending on the persons involved. He or she often uses derogatory tones and terms.

3. WHO'S YOUR BOO? The leader expects to be priority, (even over one's own family) and demands members to declare their loyalty by "choosing sides." The church leader encourages parishioners to disconnect from culture, reality, and family as it directly reflects their level of commitment to God.

4. PASTOR DON'T PLAY THAT. The leader uses public embarrassment tactics to intimidate and frighten members. Members are likely coerced into obedience for fear of public humiliation, eternal punishment or with promises of leadership roles and public recognition.

5. THE BLOODS, THE CRYPTS, & THE SAINTS. The leader strongly discourages relationships with 'unbelievers' (and often those not associated with the particular congregation) and convinces members that such relationships will be spiritually detrimental.

6. EVERYTHING IS THE DEVIL. The leadership figure will often speak of the 'world' as an inherently bad place where nothing good can ever happen. And some members may become reclusive or socially awkward.

7. BIG, FAT BULLIES. The leader often enacts his or her will through traditional, bully-like behaviors, such as stern stares, rapid hand gestures, loud noises, persistent and menacing yelling, and/or passive-aggressive behaviors including, the act of ignoring or interminable silence. The leadership figure will often tease followers by withholding approval or validation. The leader can sense desperation for his or her approval and preys on vulnerable parishioners.

8. SHOW ME THE MONEY! The leader will convince members that maintaining the pastor's and/or church's finances is more important and more spiritually sound than building one's own financial health and wealth. The leadership figure will often encourage individuals to make poor financial decisions that ultimately benefit him or her and/or the organization.

9. LADIES, FREE BEFORE 11. Predatory male leadership figures will often prey upon individuals (particularly, single women) who lack a visible, involved, invested male presence. Sexual advances are, unfortunately,

common within religiously abusive environments. Leadership figures will often use their considerable influence for sexual favors.

Black women are too willing to be manipulated and too often exchange their power for companionship. We regurgitate narrow-minded religious philosophies because being alone (even if only for a little while) is too uncomfortable. Within these deeply traditional religious settings, we are unable to realize and comfortably articulate our value. We submit to the religious bully's need to feel superior when they are otherwise invisible and sorely oppressed and transferring hate and condemnation to other black persons is their response to oppression. That energy never dies, it just recycles. Thus, the bully's feelings and experiences become more important and are given far more consideration than the feelings and experiences of the oppressed. And unfortunately, black women inadvertently become oppressors.

Our children, our mates, our co-workers often feel the sting of our oppression. And the sooner we realize church doesn't heal brokenness, *the better.* Church, is a place for community engagement, encouragement, and entertainment. Yes, entertainment. The sooner we admit that church is entertaining, *the better.* And thank you for allowing me to park here for a moment so we can be honest about Sunday mornings. The rhythmic movement, animated sermons, and lively entertainment have nothing at all to do with authentic spirituality or an organic relationship with God.

If we enjoy lively church, we should just be able to say that. We cannot define salvation or eternal forgiveness based on what we *do* in church. It often becomes an emotional experience that can offer short-term enthusiasm and inspiration. But by no means is it necessary or substantially beneficial for long-term spiritual health and wellness.

Too often this sub-culture becomes harmful to our communities because creative and critical thinking has been replaced with blind discipleship. Our interests are not being served because we'd rather clap on beat, be spat upon by preachers with no vision and bad breath, and be told to disregard earthly challenges because "heaven" is our [only] goal.

We have not learned to balance soulful expression with valuable dialogue and idea generation. The stomping of our feet and waving of our hands has seemingly replaced purposeful protest and a desire to work towards community progress.

With fervency, we bully our children into obeying misinterpreted, hyper-edited scriptures, but we discourage intellectualism. We are consumed with white Christianity, but have no appreciation for historical context or actuality. We lack self awareness, esteem and motivation because extreme indoctrination includes being erroneously reminded of our nothingness. (Many Christians embrace the idea that they are unfit to establish and maintain a relationship with God void a mediator.) We are unprepared in a world that privileges whiteness because we have become comfortable with feelings of inadequacy and have accepted them as truth.

And if there was no promise of an afterlife, an endless cycle of parading about the heavens, gazing at the celestial landscape, strolling down golden sidewalks, singing, clapping, and dancing without the threat of judgment or fatigue and without the inconvenience of gender and sexuality – would we, could we, do the right thing(s) simply because it was a service to humanity...our humanity? Are we exchanging heaven on earth for the promise of an eternal vacation package?

Why are the "pearly gates" such motivation to be 'upstanding?' And has this sales model really been successful? Can we also give God glory when we believe in ourselves and our abilities? If we are truly fashioned in God's image, isn't believing in ourselves (and our creative abilities) also believing in God? If not for fear of perpetual fire – what the *hell* are we doing this for?

We must challenge ourselves to think beyond our routine. Beyond our mother's routine. And even beyond her mother's routine. Be comfortable talking to yourself. Appreciate that voice (your voice) that has the right and ability to communicate with God, without mediation.

Worship, prayer, and communion are all profoundly personal experiences that can (and maybe should) happen in private, intimate spaces. Our gathering should resemble a celebration...of life, of hope, of one another.

*Truth be told*, we are more powerful than many of our churches and pastors have alluded to and our spiritual freedom is deeply connected to our heritage, our history, and our humanity. In fact, we are spiritually stimulated by sisterhood and kinship. We are obligated to one another, and therefore it is our right to challenge what conflicts with our intuition. It is our duty to question. It is our responsibility to be Loud.

# Chapter Twenty-Three

## Joy Comes in the Morning

*"Success is liking yourself, liking what you do, and liking how you do it."*
*— Maya Angelou*

### Dr. Jewell Winn

Even when I'm a mess, I still put on a vest with an S on my chest, says Alicia
Keys in her song 'Superwoman.' I am a strong Black woman – at least that is
what I need for you to believe. But understand this – I hurt, I cry, I am angry,
I am frustrated, I am pissed off, I hate, I am in love, I sing, I dance, I laugh, I
smile, I frown, I masturbate, I bleed, I kiss, I hug, I punch, I am beautiful, I
am ugly, I kick, I cramp, I strut, I run, I walk, I sleep, I snore – just to name a
few. Does this make me strong or weak? Does it make me successful or
unsuccessful? Some women are so affected by the 'strong Black woman or
superwoman' syndrome that their ability to be in touch with who they really
are or how they really feel is hindered.

We have read about women who tried to prove something to
somebody their entire lives—mom, dad, husband, siblings, partners, children,
bosses, etc. We read about women seeking love in all the wrong places—
when love was there all along if they had just looked UP. We read about
women who felt trapped and alone, but they have found their freedom or at
least a pathway to freedom. My grandmother used to tell me not to worry
too much about anything because joy will certainly come in the morning. I
did not understand why she would always say that because joy did not

necessarily come the next day as I anticipated, but it truly did come 'in the morning.'

This was not some magical moment that would occur—it was an awakening. I would get so deep in my valley that it did not seem like I would ever come up or ever see happiness again as I was going through my divorce. It seemed like I cried every single day leading up to my court date. I did not know how I was going to survive raising two children alone. I was raised in a two-parent household with successful parents who were engaged in the community and everybody knew them. There was an expectation that I would live what I considered the 'perfect' life—married with two children and the white picket fence. Who came up with that definition of the 'perfect' life anyway? I was trying to prove to my parents that they did an outstanding job raising me. I was trying to prove to my friends that even though I was the first one of them to get married that I would have the perfect marriage with my high school sweetheart.

I was trying to prove to my husband that he made the right choice. I was trying to prove to everybody that I was going to make this thing work no matter what. Why? In retrospect, because I did not know who I was and didn't really know who he was, even though we had dated for 10 years, my marriage failed. It was the most devastating thing that could have happened to me—I thought. Through the tears, the heartbreak, the lonely nights, the scary nights, the embarrassment, the financial struggles, and spiritual warfare —joy came in the morning.

I was not a single mother; I was a single woman. My ex-husband was the best father any woman could have dreamed of. He never deserted our kids; he paid me child support straight outta pocket without going through the 'system', he attended every event they were involved in that his schedule allowed, and he ensured them that he loved them more than anything despite what we were going through. I remarried a man who I consider my angel. He is patient, kind, forgiving, and most importantly, he loves my children as though they were his own—Joy.

Embarrassment is considered a feeling of self-consciousness, shame, or awkwardness—a feeling—something only I could control. I was not perfect and I had to realize that my mistakes, missteps and hurting other people had consequences. I had to learn to forgive myself first so that I could forgive others—Joy.

My parents provided somewhat of a privileged life for me. I drove a Corvette to high school!! We took great vacations every year. I did not know what financial aid was in college because my dad just wrote a check each semester to pay for my tuition. Life was good until I got married, got in debt, got divorced and had to make it on my own with two kids. Yes child support was provided, but I was trying to live the life that my parents provided for me —Wrong Answer. Financial challenges coupled with the emotions associated with the divorce were taking me down further in the valley. I had to realize that I was not my father—I did not have his money and I needed to live within my means. I started clipping coupons, working two jobs and being more responsible financially. Eventually, I was able to build a beautiful home for my children—Joy.

I remember how angry I was at God for taking my grandmother away. She died of stomach cancer in 1990. I thought my world was coming to an end. She was everything to me. I could talk to her about anything. No matter how bad a situation would seem, she would always find something positive to say. I never heard her say a negative word about anybody. She opened her house to everyone and she never met a stranger. So why did God take such a beautiful spirit? I was in a spiritual warfare—I questioned God, I prayed to God, I turned from God, I ran to God—confused.

One night I had a dream. My grandmother was standing over me smiling; she was so pretty and young looking. She did not look sick and had all of her beautiful hair. She touched my face and said, 'don't be mad at God anymore baby; just look at me. I'm happy. I'm not suffering anymore. I don't have to take chemo anymore. And most importantly, I can always look out for you wherever you are and whatever you do. Keep smiling and keep doing God's will.' I woke up crying uncontrollably, ran out of the house and started screaming to God that I was so sorry that I doubted Him. Then a peace came over me that I could not explain and I will never forget that day as long as I live—Joy.

So as I think about how I feel being a Black woman, I cannot help but feel all of the emotions expressed in the stories shared in this book. It has not been easy, and as I now understand, it was not supposed to be. I hope each person reading this book will find their freedom, their peace, and their joy and ultimately love. I read in my favorite book a long time ago that love bears all things, believes all things, hopes all things, and endures all things.

Be blessed!

# Chapter Twenty-Four

Saving Ourselves From Ourselves –
We Are Collective By Nature,
The Black Woman and The Black Man

*"Respect her like your mother.*
*Protect her like your daughter.*
*Love her like a wife."*
*The Thoughts of a Good Man...*

**Dr. Walter Milton, Jr.**

As the sun gave way to the moon, the night was beautifully introduced to the moment. I stared out the bay window facing the east, embracing my epoch, the dawn of my new beginning, a life without the woman who has had the most profound impact on me – my mother. It all hit me at once; I met the essence of my existence once again; losing a nephew shot to death, a sister, brother; two nieces who tragically died in a fire and my father, feeling this level of sting hurts to the core. However, when my mother died, it was a little different this time, understanding the pain of feeling the emotions while relating to that of an orphan.

The foundation of my heart yearned her voice profusely; the need to hear her voice during the raging sea of life became immensely loud. However, at that moment all I could do was embrace the storehouse of memories that she left foot printed in my soul. The most painful part of losing loved ones is the feeling that you have when you physically yearn their smile, embrace and all of their idiosyncrasies, maybe those things that may have nerved you, like my brother's snoring and his ability to yawn like no other, however, I would trade those things to have a chance to communicate with him and laugh with him. Moreover, the loss of a mother is one of the greatest lessons learned, in that you value the women of your life even more. A mother's demonstration of unconditional love is like no other.

This is a crucial time in history; serendipity is truly at play, for me, it is evident that the Creator has deemed the significance of shedding light on what appears to be a bleak situation impacting the lives of so many of our women between the gates of America. However, I believe there is a strong sense of awakening that is taking place; I see this as an opportunity to expose some of the root causes that have created challenges and critical information that can help us heal and get back on the right track, especially with our relationships and the way we treat each other; our respect level and the urgency of preparing our children for a better tomorrow. Simply put, Black men have to stand up, love support Black women to a higher standard. We have to love our women so that they feel safe and protected on every level that one can imagine.

There is a resounding voice of Black women that is yelling at the top of the mountain "know thyself and love thyself." I have learned that there is a direct correlation with knowing oneself and breaking the psychological chains that can trap and bind one into submission to conditions that control ones thoughts and behaviors. Haki Madhubuti puts it very succinctly and clearly as follows:

People Black and stone.
Be careful of that which is designated beautiful
Most of us have been taught from the basements
of other people's minds.
Often we mistake strip-mining for farming
and that that truly glows is swept under
the rug of group production.
It is accepted in America that beauty is

thin, long & the color of bubble gum.
Few articles generated by the millions are beautiful
except people.
Trust people
One by one
the darker they come
the more you can give your heart,
Their experiences most likely are yours
or will be yours.
Even within the hue and hue less
Among them are those
Who have recently lost their ability to re-call:
They can hurt you
drop you to your knees with words
much of that which blast from their mouths
is not them the offense is
they do not know that it is not them
as they rip your heart open
And reduce you to the enemy.

In the words of James Baldwin, "They saw themselves as others had seen them. They had been informed by the images made of them by those who had had the deepest necessity to despise them."

I am most certain that experiences impacting Black women collectively are spiritual, historical and cultural. Martin Luther King, Jr., once said that, "We are tied together in a garment of mutual destiny." We are a collective people who have been conditioned to operate individually because we have been taught information from others who do not necessarily have our best interest at heart. We simply need each other; Black women and Black men have to support, encourage, love, respect and show appreciation for one another.

Years ago, my mother told my siblings and me to get well acquainted with Deuteronomy, chapter 28. She said this chapter contained a great deal of wisdom as it pertains to blessings and curses and the importance of obedience to God. Now that I am a grown man, I can see as clear as day what my mother was trying to convey. She used to say that, "Everyone knows who we are, but we do not know who we are. If we had a clue, we would stand up and be the great people that we are destined to be – we have a divine responsibility to learn and value our culture."

In the words of Brother Haki R. Madhubuti, "I will say to you that we are at war and that Black men and Black women in America are being removed from the earth like loose sand in a wind storm. I will make you aware of our self-hating and hurting ways, I will glue your ears to those images you reflect, which are not being loved." Brother Madhubuti's words are powerful, his message relentless and relevant. We have learned to harm ourselves in so many ways because we have forgotten (or simply do not know) who we are…where we came from; therefore, our journey to where we are going looks challenging – but I know we will get there.

As Black men, we must be productive and intentional as it relates to loving Black women. We have to see ourselves as the keepers of our community. We have to remember that our culture is going to go as we go. Therefore, we have to lead righteously and selflessly, because so many are depending on our efforts. We have to always remember to listen to the roaring voices of our ancestors who speak to our souls, *do right by our women and children.*"

"How *does* it feel to be a Black woman?" – All I know is, *The Truth (Must) Be Told* – to know her is to love her and cherish her. She is the *True* Queen – she is the *True* Mother of Civilization! We must celebrate her existence and be attentive to her needs; we must love her unconditionally.

*Truth Be Told*, Black women are simply AMAZING!

# Reflections from the Soul

# ABOUT THE AUTHORS

Dr. Walter Milton, Jr., is a native of Rochester, New York. He earned a B.A. from the University of Albany and a M.S. from SUNY College at Brockport. He took post-graduate courses at the University of Rochester to receive his administrative certifications, including his superintendent's license. He holds a Doctorate degree in leadership and policy from the University of Buffalo. He is also a published author of *Me in the Making – One Man's Journey to Becoming a School Superintendent*, (2008) and *Why Black Men Must Save Black Boys in America's Public Schools* (2014). He served as a school superintendent for twelve years, in the states of New York, Michigan and Illinois. Dr. Milton is currently CEO of From the Heart International Educational Services. He is a focused and disciplined leader with great vision, effective communication skills and a passion for helping others. Dr. Milton is married with three sons and a daughter.

Dr. Jewell Green Winn has over thirty years of experience in education and serves Tennessee State University as Senior International Officer, Executive Director for International Programs, Deputy Chief Diversity Officer and Assistant Professor in Educational Leadership. Dr. Winn completed the Bachelor of Business Administration degree at Middle Tennessee State University, Masters of Public Administration and Doctorate of Education degrees at Tennessee State University. She is a member of several professional and social organizations such as the Phi Kappa Phi National Honor Society, the National Association of Diversity Officers in Higher Education, Women in Higher Education in Tennessee, and Alpha Kappa Alpha Sorority, Inc. She is a graduate of Leadership Nashville, the Maxine Smith Fellows Program, the Millennium Leadership Institute and the American Council on Education's Spectrum Executive Leadership Program. She is the founding Executive Director of From the Heart International Education Foundation. She is married to Timothy Winn and they have four adult children and four grandchildren.